York, Stacey, 1957–
Roots & wings

PARENT-TEACHER COLLECTION

**Affirming Culture in
Early Childhood Settings**

STACEY YORK

Toys 'n Things Press
St. Paul, Minnesota

Allen County Public Library
Ft. Wayne, Indiana

This book is dedicated to

Essie Octavia Tillery York

Marion Nicholas York

Maria Strooker Bijland

Martinus Bijland

Support funding for the production of this book was provided
by the Bush Foundation, through a grant to Resources for Child
Caring, Inc.

© 1991 by Toys 'n Things Press

All rights reserved.

Published by: Toys 'n Things Press
                 a division of Resources for Child Caring
                 450 North Syndicate, Suite 5
                 St. Paul, Minnesota 55104

Distributed by: Gryphon House
                 PO Box 275
                 Mt. Rainier, Maryland 20712

ISBN: 0-934140-63-4

Library of Congress Cataloging-in-Publication Data

York, Stacey
     Roots & wings : affirming culture in early childhood
settings / Stacey York.
          p.   cm.
     Includes bibliographical references.
     1. Education, Preschool—United States—Activity pro-
grams.   2. Intercultural education—United States—Activity
programs.   3. Curriculum planning—United States.
I. Title.   II. Title: Roots and wings.
LB1140.35.C74Y67 1991
370.19'342—dc20   91-2812

Printed in the United States of America.

Table of Contents

Chapter 4: Teaching Through the Classroom Environment 53

Chapter 5: Activities for Teaching Children About Culture 73

Chapter 6: Holidays and Celebrations 149

Chapter 7: Children's Awareness of Differences 159

Chapter 8: Culturally Responsive Care and Education 177

Chapter 9: Talking to Children About Differences 195

Photography

Pages 12, 15, 165, 172: Cleo Freelance Photography;
pages 27, 45, 54, 168, 189, 205: Frances Wardle, Ph.D.;
pages 33, 39, 65, 75, 79, 85, 89: Patricia Bickner; page
145: Charles Weber; pages 160, 181, 193, 197: Michael
Siluk; page 172: Steve and Mary Skjold Photographs.

Acknowledgments

As the task of writing this book comes to a close, I am mindful of the people and events that have allowed me to spend much of the last four years practicing and learning about multicultural education. I want to thank each of you for contributing to my development and the completion of *Roots & Wings*.

- Carol Morgaine, for greeting each return from graduate school with an open mind and a listening ear. You shared much of my early process and invited me to participate in yours.

- The University of Minnesota Child Care Center and Community Child Care Center, for providing me an opportunity to join you in developing and carrying out your anti-bias curriculum projects.

- All the teachers and directors who have attended my workshops and classes. Your questions, comments, experiences, ideas, and feedback clarified my own thinking and refined my practice.

- Barbara O'Sullivan, who asked me to write an 18-page pamphlet and decided I should write a book instead.

- Ann Lovrien, lead teacher at St. Paul Early Childhood Family Education; Sally Adams, Jane Kepke, Martha Gallegos, and Maritza Mariani, (CLUES); Sharon Henry, Southside Child Care Resource Center; and Beth and Ernie Cutting for reviewing, criticizing, and helping me improve this material.

- Louise Derman-Sparks, for your conviction, inspiration, and friendship. Your careful reading of the manuscript, straightforward detailed comments, and challenge to pay attention to the words helped bring this book together.

- Eileen Nelson, for holding my hand through the entire process and allowing me to be scared and overwhelmed. You gently prodded me to finish and, most of all, when I was so unsure, you consistently reminded me that I have my own voice and vision.

- Tim, for your initial editing and copying of the manuscript, and for putting up with my lack of presence and the many lonely evenings and weekends taken up by the book.

A Letter to the Reader:

There are only two lasting bequests
that we can leave to our children;
One is roots;
the other; wings.
—Unknown

I believe that children deserve to grow up anchored in their family and heritage. They deserve to receive all the support and strength that cultural roots offer. They are entitled to receive the sort of protection and support that wings can provide. Children must be sheltered by the wing of a caring adult from the discrimination, bias, and ethnocentrism that attempt to uproot them.

I want to help children grow their own wings and fly. With wings they can venture into the world beyond family, school, and neighborhood. They will be free to soar side by side with the many varieties of people and successfully make their way through life in a diverse world. With wings to fly, children will be empowered to reach heights beyond the anger and fear of prejudice and domination. They will have a perspective that allows them to see the discrimination and fuels the desire to shelter others by working for justice.

I, too, want roots and wings. I want to experience the strength of roots— of knowing who I am, where I come from, and what it means to be a person of my culture.

Finding cultural roots doesn't come easy. I am a white middle-class American woman. I was taught that America is the melting pot nation and that all people are the same. Until recently I never really thought about my cultural roots. I wasn't even sure I had any.

One set of my grandparents immigrated to America from Holland. Ancestors on my father's side of the family were some of the first settlers from England and Wales. They participated in the Revolutionary War. Like the majority of people living the United States, I am a Euro-American (descended from European immigrants).

If I believe the myth of the melting pot, then I say to myself none of this matters. We are all the same. But I know from my family that the Bylands and Yorks lived their lives very differently from one another. They ate different foods, cooked differently, celebrated different holidays, talked differently, and had very different ideas about money, childrearing, extended family, and religion. Often we clashed. The notion of America as a melting pot ignores these differences between individuals. It blinds me from noticing, believing, and understanding the cultural dynamics that were at play in my family. In the end, the melting pot deprives me of my cultural heritage.

I believe that by going inward and going back in time I can come to know and claim my ethnic roots. I will learn for myself what it means to be a Dutch American. Like a well-rooted tree, I will be grounded in myself. Having a cultural identity will give me the strength to fly. With wings I will go beyond myself and my experience, to look at and accept others for who they are. I will expose myself to worlds and people who are very different from me. They have been in my world all along, only I was too afraid notice them, much less to seek them out. If I did notice them, my fear got the best of me and told me to stay away or else I might get hurt (then thinking I might get hurt made me feel angry). In the past, I stayed in my safe little world, closed to all those who were not like me. Since I didn't know who I was, I could trust and accept no one.

By taking flight I gain a new perspective on myself. From the air I look down on my life, my experiences, and my attitudes, and I am able to see things differently. The wings carry me and I continue to change and grow, because once I started flying, I will never be willing to go back to the sheltered, scared life I once lived.

Roots and wings are of huge importance to me as a teacher. Who I am as a person is the same as who I am as a teacher. Even when I am silent I am modeling all of my strengths and fears for the children. My distorted ideas, biases, and fears of differences become the legacy I pass on to the children in my care.

But not anymore. If there is anything that I can do as an early childhood teacher—as an adult friend to children—I hope to leave them a legacy of roots and wings.

So I beckon all adults who share their lives with young children to dig down and find your roots, grow your wings, and take flight in your life and in your classroom so that we may leave an inheritance of human respect and justice for our children.

Stacy

CHAPTER 1

Introduction

The field of early childhood education has its own heritage that has been passed down from one teacher to the next. Teacher-training programs, professional organizations, professional magazines, and resource and referral agencies provide a formal structure that keeps our early childhood ways intact. Some say that as early childhood professionals, we have been very successful at holding onto our teaching practices, which are based on strong beliefs about what is best for young children. Other levels of education, such as elementary education, have been highly influenced by popular trends to push children to learn more and to learn it at a younger age. While we in early childhood education have managed to stand firm in some areas, other aspects of our profession are endangered by current trends and practices. This chapter reviews the professional roots, current trends, and opportunities for the future that set the stage for multicultural education in early childhood settings.

What Are Our Professional Roots?

We must know our traditions in order to keep them. An early childhood education heritage influences what we do with young children. Knowing our professional roots helps us understand current teaching practices, identify where they come from, and look toward where we, as a profession, are going. Though many people and social movements have influenced early childhood education, three main threads weave in and out of our long and rich tradition.

Humanistic Tradition

Early childhood education is strongly rooted in humanistic tradition. Believing that children are good, respecting them as people, treating them as individuals, and involving them in the learning process are key elements of good early childhood programs.

Child Development

Early childhood education has always had a close relationship to the study of child development. We have continually been open to the most recent information on child development and have attempted to apply it to programs for young children. As such, classrooms have emphasized teaching to the whole child, learning through play, and focusing on the here and now as opposed to education as a preparation for adulthood.

Social Reform

Early childhood education has also been a part of social reform. Many believe that positive early childhood experiences can improve society. Comprehensive early education programs like Head Start attempt to better the lives of children by counteracting the effects of poverty. Quality day care programs allow women to participate in the work force without harming the family or children's development.

You see things; and you say, 'Why?'
But I dream things that never were;
and I say, 'Why not?'
—*George Bernard Shaw*

Today: A Global Approach

A vision for society's future begins today. Recent changes in other countries suggest that Americans no longer need to live in fear of war with Russia and Eastern Europe. Instead, as a country, we must learn how to relate to and work with these people who were once considered our enemies.

Just as worldwide changes are bringing international cultures together, the influx of immigrants and refugees over the past ten years reminds us that America is a country of many cultures and languages. Our country was built on diversity, and diversity will continue to be our strength. As early childhood educators, we must recognize cultural differences and provide children with an early education experience that prepares them to live in a culturally diverse country and a peaceful, cooperative world.

Support for Multicultural Education

The time is right for multicultural education. Our largest and most influential professional organization, the National Association for the Education of Young Children (NAEYC), is actively promoting multicultural education. Early childhood programs seeking accreditation by the National Academy of Early Childhood Programs must show that they meet certain criteria regarding multicultural education. Two years ago, NAEYC published *Anti-Bias Curriculum*, a curriculum guide of developmentally appropriate activities to empower children. In addition, both the Center Accreditation Project criteria and the work on anti-bias curriculum by the staff at Pacific Oaks College in California are raising the awareness of teachers to the appropriateness of multicultural education in the early years.

Current Barriers

Just as trends within the field bring attention to multicultural education, conditions within the early childhood community make implementing multicultural education very difficult.

State Licensing Standards. State licensing standards require relatively little in the way of teacher training: Twelve credits or 90 hours of coursework are common minimum requirements for day care teachers. This means that teacher-training programs must focus on the basics such as child development, health and safety, room arrangement, daily routine, and curriculum activities. Knowledge of multicultural education, such as learning how to work with parents, is an "extra" that we supposedly pick up along the way and on our own time.

"Recipe Book" Approach. The second problem limiting the growth of multicultural education within the field is that teachers are "doers." Most early childhood teachers I know like hands-on activities and make-it/take-it workshops. Few of us have paid planning time. We plan curriculum while sitting on the floor in the doorway of a darkened classroom during nap time, in the evening while watching TV, or on Sunday afternoons. When it comes to curriculum books, we like "recipe books" that make curriculum planning quick and easy. It is difficult, if not impossible, to water down the concepts of multicultural education into a fun, how-to book without destroying their true meaning. In order for multicultural education to catch on, teachers will need to put forth extra effort to read, attend workshops, and reflect on their own teaching practices. This is asking a lot, but just think of it as a gift to children and families, and an investment in both ourselves and the children we share our lives with.

Animated Curriculum and Classrooms. Ask a teacher why she does certain activities and the answer will likely be, "They're fun, the kids love 'em, and the parents think they're so cute." We want children to have fun and enjoy themselves, but we must remember that we are in the education business and not the entertainment business (Katz 1977).

An overemphasis on entertainment has resulted in classrooms full of movie characters, cartoon characters, and TV characters. Walls are covered with murals depicting the antics of animal characters. Classrooms and groups of children are identified by cartoon mascots. Unit themes focus on cartoons and children "learn" about the theme by coloring in ditto sheets of their favorite character. Perhaps this is a commentary on the power of the media and our desire to create a mythology, a common culture. Cartoon characters and popular movies are something most of us have experienced. It is something we all have in common.

At conferences teachers swarm display booths that sell cartoon-character paraphernalia such as stickers, pencils, erasers, bulletin-board kits, finger puppets, decorated attendance charts, and calendars.

Likewise, some of the most popular early childhood curriculum books are comic books. There is even a set of such comic books for teaching children about other cultures. Each book provides monthly holiday activities. For example, children learn about the Dutch by coloring a ditto sheet of a Dutch girl in her traditional costume, cutting out a windmill and putting it together with a paper fastener, and cutting out a wooden shoe and pinning it up on the bulletin board. These books were so popular at a recent state conference that they were back ordered for months!

Children need a break from the pretend, animated world of the media. They deserve to learn about real people through meaningful activities. We need to overcome these current trends that keep our profession from affirming diversity and culture. We must go back to teaching children about the real world in order to maintain the integrity of early childhood education.

Rooted in the Early Childhood Tradition

This book is rooted in good early childhood education practices: considering the child's development, teaching through a well-organized classroom,

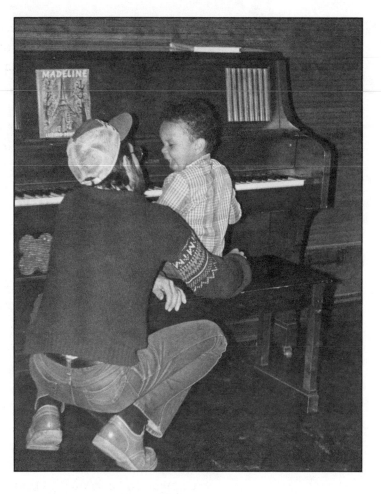

providing large blocks of time for free choice play, introducing materials, asking open-ended questions to encourage thinking and problem-solving, affirming children for their individuality and uniqueness in order to foster self-esteem, and coaching children in the way they treat one another to build social skills.

In recent years, early childhood teachers have wanted and needed resources for incorporating multicultural education into the curriculum. Unfortunately, many of the books and materials available advocate teaching elementary school level information or using methods that stunt children's development.

I hope that the ideas and information in this book give each of you wings to fly, and that by reading this book, you will feel empowered to incorporate new materials and activities into your classroom. I also hope that some of my ideas will inspire you to create many new ideas of your own.

About This Book

This book was written for early childhood teachers, program directors, teacher trainers, and parents with the following four goals in mind:

1. This book will introduce multicultural education in a simple and organized way.

2. Many practical ideas for implementing multicultural education in early childhood settings will be presented.

3. This book will spread the word about multicultural education. Good, useful information about multicultural education for young children has been available for the past ten years, but it has been "hidden" from the mainstream, appearing only in textbooks and professional journals.

4. Early childhood educators will have an alternative to the tourist approach, and will discover ways to incorporate the newest thinking about multicultural education into their classrooms.

Assumptions

The information and topics covered in *Roots & Wings* reflect child development theory, established early childhood education practices, and current accreditation standards. The decision to emphasize some information about multicultural education and leave out other information is a product of my values, my awareness and thinking, and the limitations of space and time.

This book does not include everything there is to know about multicultural education for young children. The following assumptions are not discussed in this book, but I want you to know that I believe in them, and that they are important to me. These assumptions greatly influence my perspective on multicultural education.

1. In its fullest expression, multicultural education includes addressing the issues of discrimination against individuals in all areas, including religion, gender, economic class, age, ability, and sexual preference. I have chosen to focus on culture, ethnicity, and race because so few early childhood programs deal with this issue with any success. I believe that if a program can successfully incorporate multicultural values, it can go on to incorporate the other equally important components of diversity.

2. Life in the United States is not fair for everyone. All kinds of discrimination keep individuals from having equal access to society's services and opportunities.

3. Education is not neutral. Schools and day care centers are institutions, and as such, they are part of the social structure that discriminates against individuals. As part of the social structure, early childhood programs usually teach and perpetuate white Euro-American, middle-class values. In the classroom, teachers pass on their values to children through their choice of bulletin-board displays, toys, activities, celebrations, unit themes, and interaction with the children.

4. Education can influence social change. Some politicians would like us to believe that education makes or breaks a nation and determines society's future. Unfortunately, this is not true. Politicians, influenced by industry and economics, direct education. As a result, the education of children is designed and funded to perpetuate the prevailing societal myths and to keep the country operating as it has always operated. Education, by its position in a capitalistic economy, cannot bring about social change. It cannot end prejudice and oppression. But education can influence the lives of the people it serves and the power structures within the system.

5. The process is the product. If you come to this book focused solely on the outcome of having a multicultural curriculum, you won't be open to the possibility of discovery and personal growth. Put aside your preconceived notions of what multicultural education should be and your worries about implementing it in your program. As you read this book, focus on the here and now. Open yourself up to your feelings. Take in the information bit by bit. Ask questions, stop for reflection, watch others around you, gather some materials and create some activities, and talk with children and parents. As you do these things, you will create a greater understanding of yourself, culture, and multicultural curriculum, and you will have begun the steps toward implementing multicultural education in your classroom.

> *The warrior has the wisdom to approach each event as it is,*
> *not knowing its outcome. Not forcing results.*
> *His "don't know" is the joy and courage that fill his life.*
> —*Stephen Levine*

Important Terms

It is impossible to talk about multicultural education without using specific words that relate to culture. The following terms are defined here according to the way they are used throughout the book. Read through the list. Which words are familiar to you? Which words are new? Which words name something you can relate to or have experienced in your own life?

Acculturation. The transfer of culture from one ethnic group to another. The dominant culture usually forces its values, language, and behavior on less dominant cultures. As a result, the members of the nondominant culture change their values, the way they speak, and the way they act in order to fit in and be accepted by the dominant culture.

Bias. Showing favorites or dislikes because of an inclination or point of view; the tendency to favor one ethnic group over another, or the tendency to dislike, distrust, and be afraid of a person from a particular ethnic group.

Culture. The behavior, values, beliefs, language, traits, artifacts, and products shared by and associated with a group of people. These characteristics are passed from one generation to the next through experiences and education.

Discrimination. The practice of giving different treatment to a person based on race, sex, religion, ethnicity, age, mental capacity, physical ability, and/or sexual preference.

Dominant culture. The ruling or prevailing culture exercising authority or influence. In the United States, the dominant culture is the white, Euro-American middle class. More specifically, white, upper-class men dominate the leadership and decision-making positions and they benefit most from living in our society. Within the dominant culture, there are differences of participation in and benefits from mainstream society based on a person's gender and economic class.

Ethnic. Refers to the commonality among people because of their ancestors; it includes race, religion, national origin, physical traits, values, beliefs, customs, language, and lifestyle.

Ethnocentrism. The belief that one's culture or country is better than other cultures and countries; judging other countries and cultures from one's own point of view and expecting them to act and think the same way.

Euro-American. A Caucasian person living in America of European, Scandinavian, Slavic, or Mediterranean descent.

Minority. A group of people with a separate identity and a lower status from the dominant society. Minorities may or may not have fewer people than the dominant group, known as the majority.

Oppression. Unjust and cruel use of authority to harm a person and keep that person from having access to society's benefits.

Prejudice. Having a preconceived judgement or opinion without accurate knowledge or reason; an irrational attitude against a group of people and their characteristics.

Racism. Belief that one race is better than another and using that belief as the basis for dominating people.

Stereotype. An oversimplified and unvarying idea about the characteristics of members of a group.

Organization

Roots & Wings introduces you to multicultural education and takes you through the process of implementing multicultural education in early childhood settings. The book is divided into three sections: introduction to multicultural education, implementing multicultural education in early childhood settings, and the interpersonal effects of culture.

Chapter 2 answers the question "What is multicultural education?" by defining it and by providing an overview of the five main approaches. It also includes definitions of common terms associated with multicultural education.

The midsection of the book addresses curriculum. Chapter 3 is the most important chapter because it takes you through the step-by-step process of developing a multicultural curriculum in an early childhood setting. Chapter 4 provides guidelines and practical ideas for incorporating diversity in the classroom. Chapter 5 answers concerns about what to teach young children and how to teach it. It contains over 50 activities, 12 unit themes, and a curriculum planning form. Chapter 6 helps teachers understand the role of holidays in early childhood education and offers guidelines for making celebrations a positive experience. It even includes a calendar of multicultural holidays.

The final three chapters focus on the interpersonal effects of culture. Chapter 7 discusses the differences young children notice, how prejudice is formed, and why children are pre-prejudiced. Chapter 8 highlights the influence of culture on families. Teachers will find this a helpful resource for working with and understanding minority families and including parents in the program. Chapter 9 focuses on communication between teachers and children. Early childhood teachers often find it difficult to talk with children about sensitive topics, answer their pointed questions, and challenge their discriminatory remarks.

You may want to read the book in sequence chapter by chapter. If you want answers to specific concerns, read the first three chapters to get a basic understanding of multicultural education. Then read the chapters and sections that meet your specific needs.

Questions to Ponder

1. What people, theories, or life experiences have influenced what you do with young children?
2. What are your dreams for society? What impact do you want to have on children, families, or society?
3. What are your assumptions about multicultural education for young children?

Resources and References

Derman-Sparks, Louise. *Anti-Bias Curriculum*. Washington, DC: NAEYC, 1989.

Feeney, Stephanie, Doris Christensen, and Eva Moravcik. *Who Am I in the Lives of Children?* Columbus: Merrill, 1987.

Freire, Paulo. *Pedagogy of the Oppressed*. New York: Continuum, 1970.

Katz, Lillian. *Talks With Teachers*. Washington, DC: NAEYC, 1977.

Levine, Stephen. *Who Dies?* Garden City, N.Y.: Anchor Books, 1982.

Morrison, George S. *Early Childhood Education Today*. Columbus: Merrill, 1988.

National Academy of Early Childhood Programs. *Guide to Accreditation*. Washington, DC: NAEYC, 1985.

Sevaly, Karen. *December Idea Book*. Moreno Valley, CA: Teacher's Friend Publications, 1986.

Shor, Ira, and Paulo Freire. *A Pedagogy For Liberation*. South Hadley, MA: Bergin and Garvey, 1987.

Weber, Evelyn. *Ideas Influencing Early Childhood Education: A Theoretical Analysis*. New York: Teachers College Press, 1984.

回回回回回回回回回回回回回回回回回回回回回回

What Is Multicultural Education?

Ask five people to define multicultural education and you're sure to get five different answers. Multicultural education can be confusing because it means different things to different people; it is complicated by many definitions, a variety of approaches, and a number of terms that describe its many aspects. This chapter will help you sort things out by examining the nature of multicultural education, listing its goals, and explaining its five basic approaches. Let's begin the journey into the world of multicultural education by asking some basic questions.

What Is Culture?

You may not be convinced that culture has a large influence on children or your classroom. Let's begin by defining culture. Try this activity. List everything you can think of that constitutes culture or that is related to culture. Compare your list to the list in the box. Does culture influence family life? You bet it does!

Culture is things, customs, and values. Culture can be thought of in terms of the concrete items and objects we see, hold, and use. Items like clothing, artwork, food, and dance are tangible symbols of a person's culture. Culture is also experienced in how people live out their lives as well as what they believe and what values they hold dear. Family roles, childrearing patterns, communication styles, and holiday traditions are ways in which culture influences how we as individuals live our daily lives. Finally, people's goals in life and their beliefs about human nature and humanity are invisible but ever present aspects of cultures.

Culture List

Things (cultural objects)	Customs (how people live)	Values (beliefs, reasons for actions)
clothing	celebrations	spirituality, religion
jewelry	holidays	role of people in world
food	marriage	role of children
furniture	how people communicate	role of environment
art	who lives in families	attitude toward time
music	age of adulthood	attitude toward money
dance	recreation	definition of achievement
language	family roles	understanding of world
games	child care	
houses	how people show affection	

Adapted from an activity in *Alerta: A Multicultural, Bilingual Approach to Teaching Young Children* by Leslie R. Williams and Yvonne De Gaetano. Menlo Park: Addison-Wesley, 1985.

What Does Multicultural Education Include?

Multicultural education includes teaching children about their own culture—their ethnic heritage. It also means exposing children to other cultures and helping them be comfortable with and respect all the ways people are different from each other. It is teaching children how to relate to one another and how to play fair. Multicultural education encourages children to notice and think about unfairness, and challenges them to do something about the unfairness toward people in their world.

Multicultural education is more than teaching information directly. It means providing a classroom that includes materials depicting people from many different places doing many different things. It's creating and maintaining an environment that says everyone is welcome here. It is also encouraging children to act, think, and talk like members of their own culture. It's helping children to like themselves just the way they are. It's encouraging children to actively explore a variety of materials and exposing them to experiences that might not be part of their daily life experience.

Why is Multicultural Education Important?

The Center Accreditation Project has identified multicultural education as one component of a quality early childhood program. We, as early childhood teachers, know that quality programs produce positive outcomes for children, families, and society as a whole. Yet many of us still do not understand why multicultural education is so important in the early years.

Encourages a True Sense of Self

Multicultural education is important for young children because they deserve to be in programs where it is safe for them to be who they are. Children deserve to know the truth about themselves, the real world, and the people in it. Children have the right to feel good about themselves, to learn to be courageous, and not to feel like victims. Children are entitled to their cultural heritage and to be proud of it.

Promotes Development

Early childhood teachers know that these years are an important time for children's growth and development. During this time, children acquire a self-concept, build their self-esteem, learn how to make friends, become aware of family and community, learn to use words to express themselves, have strong feelings and fears, use magical (and often distorted) thinking, and tend to believe everything they see and hear. These characteristics and developmental milestones result in pre-prejudiced thinking and behavior. Consequently, this is the time to help children move ahead in their thinking and learn to function successfully and cooperatively in a culturally diverse society and world.

Prepares for the Future

Multicultural education is important because the world is changing. As teachers, we are preparing children to live in the future. By the year 2000, one third of all the people living in the United States will be people of color. We will experience living in a society made up of many people from many different cultures.

Prevents Isolation

When I taught in and directed suburban and rural programs, I often wondered if multicultural education was relevant because all of the children in my program seemed the same. Since then, I've learned that multicultural education is just as important in an "all-white" program or an "all-Hispanic program" as it is in a multiracial program.

Growing up in a community where everyone is the same can give children the false impression that everyone everywhere is alike. Children in monocultural communities and monocultural early childhood programs can grow up not knowing about other cultures, without developing a sensitivity to the life experiences of others, and without ever thinking about people of other cultures. Unfortunately, these children don't know that their country and the world is made up of many communities that are very different from their own. Excluding multicultural education from the early childhood curriculum is to risk isolating children from the rest of the world.

Discourages Denial and Fear of Differences

Children in monocultural environments risk growing up denying or being afraid of the differences among people. It's common to hear teachers in rural or suburban programs say, "I never knew there were differences." "My family never talked about them." "In a small town it's different because everyone is the same and everyone is accepted." "I'm afraid to go into the city because of all the killings and rapes."

An early childhood program that doesn't provide multicultural education encourages denial and teaches children a narrow view of the world. Teaching as if there was only one perspective that really matters promotes the idea that other ways of being in the world are deficient and deviant. Euro-American children need to understand and accept that there are other perspectives and other ways of being in the world.

Cultivates Acceptance

When I lived in a small town people noticed and talked about differences. Sometimes it was just gossip, but other times the differences were used to put someone down or make us feel superior. People talked about what church you attended, what side of the railroad tracks you lived on, what you farmed, where you bought your seed, where you worked, what kind of truck you drove, what make of farm machinery you used, where you went on vacation, who was married and who was single, who stayed in town and who left. To teach multicultural education in classes where everyone seems the same, begin with the differences at hand. Even programs in which everyone seems to be the same can emphasize differences among the children such as hair color, family size, where they live, and where their parent(s) work.

Goals of Multicultural Education

Goals describe the desired outcome. As a result of offering multicultural education I hope that you, as an adult working with young children, will have the opportunity to experience each of these goals.

- Recognize the beauty, value, and contribution of each child.
- Foster high self-esteem and a positive self-concept in children.
- Teach children about their own culture.
- Introduce children to other cultures.

- Provide children with a positive experience exploring similarities and differences.
- Encourage children to respect other cultures.
- Increase children's ability to talk to and play with people who are different from them.
- Help children to be a group member.
- Talk about racism and current events regularly with children.
- Help children live happily and cooperatively in a diverse world.
- Help children notice and do something about unfair behavior and events.

Types of Multicultural Education

Christine Sleeter and Carl Grant examined 60 books and 200 articles on multicultural education in order to understand how multicultural education is taught in America. As a result, they identified five different approaches to multicultural education: human relations, single group studies, multicultural, anti-bias, and bilingual/bicultural approach. Each of the approaches was developed between the 1960s and the late 1980s and generated its own assumptions, goals, content, and methods. At this time we really don't know if one approach is more effective than another because there have been no research studies that compare the effects of different multicultural education programs on children's development and learning (Sleeter and Grant 1987). While their research focuses on methods used in kindergarten through twelfth-grade programs, it is still applicable to early childhood education. I have attempted to translate their descriptions of elementary school practices into common early childhood learning experiences. Think of your program and your curriculum as you examine each approach.

Human Relations Approach

This approach focuses on teaching children how to make and maintain good relationships with children of different ethnic groups. The human relations approach emphasizes the development of a positive self-concept and skills in forming and maintaining friendships. It focuses on the importance of appreciating each other, talking to one another, and learning how to get along with one another. Children learn about similarities and differences, and that name-calling hurts people's feelings. Curriculum themes such as "I'm Me and I'm Special," "Let's Be Friends," and "Alike and Different" are examples of a human relations approach to multicultural education.

Single Group Studies

This method is based on the belief that knowing oneself is the beginning of understanding and accepting others. Single group studies are especially popular at the college level with departments and entire degree programs such as African American studies, Latin American studies, Scandinavian studies, and women's studies. The goals of single group studies are to teach appreciation of one's own culture, to raise cultural awareness, and to encourage individuals to take action on behalf of their people. The curriculum includes learning about the historical influences, cultural patterns, and current issues that influence or affect the culture.

Sleeter and Grant outline the content of an African American history class. According to them, it might include topics such as the African roots, economics of the slave trade, American slavery, the Emancipation Proclamation, Black protest, Black leadership, integration and segregation, and Black power today. In an early childhood setting, children would learn about themselves, their cultural heritage, their cultural community, and heroes from their culture. This approach might be particularly useful in a setting that serves one particular culture such as an all-African American program.

Unfortunately many Euro-American programs and multiracial programs have turned this model into another form of classroom entertainment. Consequently, children learn about cultures through units or themes that focus on one group of people at a time. Hawaii Week, Africa Week, Mexico Week, and Indian Week are examples of learning about cultures one at a time. This method is often called the "tourist" approach because it's like taking a short trip. For a brief period of time the class goes sight-seeing, trying out and enjoying the food, the folk costumes, exotic dances, and music of each culture. At the end of the week the class leaves the country and the topic is dropped until the same time next year. The tourist approach does little to meet the goals of the single studies approach. It can hinder children by reinforcing the idea that people who are different from them lived a long time ago and all they do is wear funny clothes, eat weird food, and dance.

Multicultural Education

This approach advocates that America is like a "tossed salad" and that the strength of our society comes from diversity. Multicultural education provides children with the message that it is all right to be different, differences are good, and people deserve to choose how they want to live. This approach also affirms equality: people deserve the same opportunities regardless of gender, race, class, religion, age, ability, or sexual preference. Programs using this approach are nondiscriminatory and show respect for children's families, home life, and learning style. Children learn about the contributions and characteristics of the cultures represented in their classroom or community. They may also be encouraged to use more than one language. The classroom materials and bulletin boards reflect all types of diversity. Units on boys and girls, families, bodies, and celebrations are examples of themes that affirm diversity.

Anti-Bias Education

This approach focuses on changing inequality and the sources of stereotypes. Anti-bias education prepares people to change the social structures that perpetuate injustice. Whereas the other approaches assume that changing people's attitudes will eventually change the social structure, an anti-bias approach is built on the belief that if the structures change, people's attitudes will change. As a result, students are taught to take action against the inequalities present in society.

Anti-bias classrooms attempt to model democracy. Teachers include children in decision-making and any changes such as rearranging the room. Children make choices, are encouraged to act on their choices, and are given opportunities to work cooperatively. They are taught skills in individual and group problem-solving and critical thinking, and they are provided with experiences in taking social action.

Louise Derman-Sparks sites an example from a preschool classroom. A boy's father had difficulty visiting his son's class because he was handicapped. The school provided no handicap parking spaces, so the class made a handicap parking space in the school parking lot. This illustrates how the curriculum is based on and emerges from the daily lives of the children, incidents that take place in the classroom, and current world events.

Bicultural/Bilingual Education

Bilingual education uses many methods to teach English to non-English-speaking children. Bicultural programs encourage children to maintain and take pride in their roots while learning to adapt to the dominant culture.

Some teaching methods are respectful of children's native languages and customs. Other bilingual education methods require children to drop their first language altogether by immersing them in English-speaking classrooms.

Studies indicate that minority people are the most successful when they can communicate with and understand the dominant culture, and can communicate with and know the ways of their own culture. This is the essence of being bicultural—being able to successfully live in two worlds. Early childhood programs that serve non-English-speaking children can help these children learn to function in and between their two cultures.

Bilingual education focuses on teaching the dominant language (English) and the accepted ways of being in society to children of minority cultures. The emphasis is on helping minority, low-income, and non-English-speaking children become acculturated into the dominant society as quickly as possible. Then, everyone living in this country will identify with and share the dominant culture. In other words, we will have a "melting pot" rather than a "tossed salad."

Choosing an Approach

Approaches to multicultural education vary greatly. As a guideline, Sleeter and Grant suggest trying one approach at a time. They say you can even combine two approaches and still give adequate attention to the goals and methods of each approach. For example, you might combine the human relations approach with multicultural education. This may be the place to start, since many early childhood programs already do a good job of emphasizing self-esteem and socialization.

Avoid dabbling in multicultural education. Taking a little bit from here and a little bit from there will only confuse both you and the children. Some approaches are incompatible with early childhood education. The single group studies approach is inappropriate for early childhood settings because it becomes a tourist approach when adapted for young children. Tourist activities that focus on food, music, dances, and costumes emphasize stereotypes and contradict the goals of both multicultural and anti-bias education.

This book is written from a multicultural perspective that incorporates anti-bias values. A number of activities that fall under the human relationship approach are also included. Due to limits of time and space the focus is exclusively on culture.

Conclusion

By now you are probably developing your own definition of multicultural education. I hope that reading about the five different approaches has you thinking about your own group of children, activities you've tried in the past, and possibilities for the future. Once you identify an approach or two, you can write goals for the project. Use the list of goals in this chapter as a starting point. Finally, refer back to the definition of terms to clarify ideas discussed in the following chapters.

Questions to Ponder

1. How would you define multicultural education?
2. Why is multicultural education important to you?
3. Which of the five approaches to multicultural education fits with your beliefs?
4. Which of the five approaches best matches what is currently taking place in your classroom?

Resources and References

Derman-Sparks, Louise. *Anti-Bias Curriculum*. Washington, DC: NAEYC, 1989.

Grant, Carl A., and Christine E. Sleeter. *Turning on Learning: Five Approaches for Multicultural Teaching Plans for Race, Class, Gender, and Disability*. Columbus: Merrill, 1989.

Hernandez, Hilda. *Multicultural Education: A Teacher's Guide to Content and Process*. Columbus: Merrill, 1989.

Sleeter, Christine E., and Carl A. Grant. "An Analysis of Multicultural Education in the U.S.A." *Harvard Educational Review* 57 (1987): 421-44.

———. *Making Choices for Multicultural Education*. Columbus: Merrill, 1988.

CHAPTER 3

Implementing Multicultural Education

"Where do I start?" is a question I ask when I'm feeling overwhelmed. Perhaps I've dumped the contents of the storage closet onto the floor and now it's time to sort it out, reorganize, give stuff away, and put things back. Or maybe I've spent the evening baking and now the kitchen is turned upside down—dirty pots, pans, and baking ingredients are everywhere. So I survey the mess and decide to walk away for a bit in order to gather some energy to tackle the mess.

"Where do we start?" is often the first question asked by teachers eager to implement multicultural education in their classroom. I suggest that you begin by being curious: approach this awesome (and mind-boggling) task with every bit of curiosity that you can muster. The questions you ask will give you clues about what you know and don't know, about your needs, interests, and fears.

Understanding the Process

The early childhood teachers with whom I've worked raise many important questions, especially when first starting out. Here are some of them:

- How do we incorporate diversity into a program where everyone is the same?
- How do we move away from focusing on celebrations?
- What are age-appropriate multicultural activities?
- How do we deal with the resistance, fear, and anger of staff and parents?
- How can we make multicultural education a real part of our lives, so that it becomes an attitude?
- How can we move from multicultural education to anti-bias education?
- How can we do it without forcing it on people?

- How can we take into account people's different levels of interest and awareness?
- How much effect do we really have on children's development of prejudiced behavior?
- How do we learn about this stuff?
- What are the parents going to say about all of this?
- How is this going to change *me*?

These questions illustrate how complex and overwhelming multicultural education can be. There are so many things to think about and so many people's feelings to consider, not to mention little time and money available for implementation. So take a step back and allow yourself to feel the size of the task. Allow yourself to be awed and amazed, scared or overwhelmed, and finally, excited and full of anticipation. As you have these feelings, keep the following suggestion in mind:

Allow Plenty of Time

Give yourself one to five years of experimenting with materials and activities, responding to children, and talking with parents. In other words, a two-hour staff inservice or reading one book will not result in instant multicultural education in the classroom.

Start Where You Are

The only place to start is where you are in your development as a teacher, using what you already know and have experienced. It is impossible to make one giant leap from the "tourist" approach to the anti-bias approach.

Change "Things" First

It is easier to change things than it is to change people. Start by changing the things in your classroom like bulletin boards, books, toys, learning activities, and celebrations. This gives you some time to develop greater self-awareness, reflect on attitudes, collect activity ideas, and learn communication skills (Prescott 1984).

Find Support

You can't do it alone. Teachers who try to implement multicultural education by themselves end up feeling alienated, defensive, hurt, and burned out. Two years ago I taught child development at a suburban technical college. The school district observed Martin Luther King, Jr.'s birthday by dismissing the students from school and requiring the teachers to spend the day in inservice. During the two-hour lunch break, a movie about the life of Dr. King was shown in the lecture hall. I was the only person to attend. I sat in that hall all by myself watching the film. Even the staff development coordinator failed to attend. She had the janitor start and stop the film. I knew then just how alone I was in trying to change the curriculum and teaching practices within that institution. I quit at the end of the year feeling very alienated and disillusioned.

Talk About What You Are Doing

We aren't used to talking with our coworkers about multicultural issues, cultural heritage, or ideas for multicultural education, but we must keep talking about it, or it will fade away. People in our society are most comfortable ignoring differences and being silent about prejudice. As a result, staff may attend an evening inservice session on multicultural education, but when they see each other the next day, no one mentions the experience.

Instead, when a staff person attends a class in the community or reads an article on multicultural education, ask them to share it with the entire staff at the next staff meeting. When planning curriculum, ask, "What are we going to do next month that includes multicultural values?" The momentum needed to make programmatic changes will quickly dwindle unless we keep multicultural education in the forefront by putting forth an effort to talk about the issues and our experiences.

Expect to Make Mistakes

Implementing multicultural education is an opportunity to confront your need to be perfect. It is a lesson in pioneering and charting new territory. You may have an idea of what you want to accomplish as a teacher, but understand that the journey is full of peaks and valleys, blind curves, unexpected obstacles, and unanticipated rewards. Embrace the mistakes as proof that you are alive as a teacher, taking risks and trying new things. Hooray for you!

Introducing Multicultural Education

Since multicultural education is a complex, confusing, and controversial subject, it is important that the entire staff be involved from the beginning. If you are the one in charge of introducing multicultural education, start by bringing the staff together to share their questions and concerns. Set aside at least two hours for this introductory session.

Find a Facilitator and a Recorder

One person, perhaps yourself, needs to take the initiative and responsibility for setting the meeting date and time, finding a location, gathering the materials, and facilitating the meeting. Open the meeting with a brief presentation about the need for multicultural awareness in early childhood settings. Help participants feel welcome by making it clear that you have come together to explore the possibilities, and that this meeting is not to convince or trick people into adding multicultural curriculum to their teaching responsibilities.

You may also want to ask someone to take notes of the meeting. Afterwards, combine the notes with any information you might have presented (or the group generated), type all this up, and distribute a copy to everyone on the staff.

Begin with Questions

Once you have set the tone for the session, use brainstorming as a technique to generate questions about multicultural education. Ask someone to write the questions on large sheets of chart paper for all to see. Classify them into broad categories. Then break up into small groups, assigning a category of questions and concerns to each small group for discussion. End this portion of the meeting by asking the small groups to share the highlights of their discussion with the large group. Note the main points for future reference.

Explore the Nature of the Task

Next, discuss the question, "What is multicultural education?" Again, list all the answers on large sheets of paper so everyone can see them. Ask people to take a moment to read the opening paragraphs of this chapter about the complexity and overwhelming nature of multicultural education. Affirm one another's fears, reservations, concerns, and excitement.

Identify the Approaches

Follow the initial discussion with a mini-lecture on the five approaches to multicultural education. Break up into small groups and discuss the questions at the end of Chapter 2. Ask the small groups to report back to the whole group. Depending on the conversation, you may want to choose one or two approaches to explore further at a future meeting.

Create a Vision of the Future

So far, you have explored the concept of multicultural education, identified the major approaches, and talked about your fears and concerns. Now it is time to move a step closer to taking action. Hand out the form, *Envisioning Multicultural Education In Our Program*, giving participants 15 minutes to fill it out. Afterwards, bring everyone back together to identify the present situation, the positive and negative forces, and the people who would be affected by a multicultural curriculum. Ask each person to share a vision for the future and write the visions on chart paper for all to see. As a group, attempt to write a vision statement using the individual descriptions.

Identify Action Steps

Develop goals from the vision statement and brainstorm the steps you would need to take in order to implement multicultural education in your program. Next, sequence the steps in the order they would most likely occur. Make loose plans to achieve those steps, such as setting up a committee or a follow-up meeting.

Bring the Meeting to a Close

End the introductory session with a discussion about change. Ask each person to reflect on the question, "How do you deal with change?" Encourage participants to share their responses with the group. Talk about how people respond differently to change and how you might anticipate problems associated with change. Follow up the meeting by distributing notes of the introductory session to all program staff.

Envisioning Multicultural Education in Our Program

Complete this worksheet individually or in small groups to help you create a vision of how you want your program to be in the future. Come together as a staff to share your ideas and discuss the current state (and possible future) of multicultural education in your program.

1. Describe the current role of multicultural education in your program.

2. Describe the forces that will help your program improve or add multicultural education.

3. Describe the forces that hold you back from improving or adding multicultural education.

4. Who will be affected by adopting or improving multicultural education?

5. Describe your vision for the future regarding multicultural education.

6. What steps must you take to incorporate or improve multicultural education?

Adapted from the "Ice House" exercise in *Resource Manual for a Living Revolution* by Virginia Coover and others. Philadelphia: New Society Publishers, 1987.

A Note About Change

Some people avoid it at all cost. These folks may become silent and show signs of resistance by not attending meetings or failing to follow through with assignments. Others try to avoid dealing with change by rationalizing: "But we've always done it this way, and it works. Why mess up a good thing?" Some try to put it off, if at all possible. "This is a really busy year for me. I'm working on other things. How about next year?" Luckily, there are folks around who thrive on diversity and welcome new opportunities with open arms. These people can provide the motivating energy to help the rest of the staff.

Multicultural Education Begins with Empowerment

As a teacher, you may arrive on the doorstep of multicultural education unaware of your own culture and family history, in denial of your own prejudice and oppression, confused about how to teach young children multicultural concepts, afraid of experiencing conflict and the anger of parents, ambivalent about putting extra energy into such a project, and resistant to change in either yourself or your activities with children. As a result, you may want to work toward achieving the following personal goals as you implement multicultural education:

Goals for Teachers

1. Increase your awareness of personal assumptions and your attitudes toward diversity.
2. Increase your understanding of "-isms" and prejudice.
3. Increase your awareness of prevailing social values and how they show up in education.
4. Notice, identify, and remove stereotypic materials from your classroom.
5. Display and set out nonstereotypic multicultural materials in your classroom.
6. Plan and carry out developmentally appropriate, multicultural activities with your children.
7. Initiate and participate in casual conversations with your children about topics related to multicultural education and diversity.
8. Respond to children's biased remarks and actions.
9. Initiate and carry out activities with children that question and take action against injustice.
10. Interact with the children's families in authentic, respectful ways.

Teachers Need Empowerment

Teachers need to be empowered. We need to feel confident in who we are, what we know, and what we can do. We need to be respected for who we are as individuals and where we are in our own journey as professionals. We need a safe place in which to ask questions, share hard feelings, and make mistakes. We need a supportive yet challenging setting that will encourage us to ask questions, reflect on our assumptions, analyze why we believe the way we do, and explore how society influences our personal beliefs.

Steps to Empowerment

Through empowerment, teachers gain awareness of issues and the self-confidence that is needed to carry out a multicultural curriculum. The following diagram shows the progression teachers go through when implementing multicultural education in an early childhood setting.

> Achieve goals of multicultural education.

> Reflect on attempts to incorporate multicultural education into the program, solve problems, and revise methods.

> Change the environment, offer multicultural activities, and talk with children about diversity.

> Establish or renew belief in and commitment to multicultural education. Set project goals.

> Increase awareness of personal experiences, attitudes, biases, and societal oppression.

> Bring to the project knowledge of child development, early childhood education practices, and experience as an early childhood teacher.

The Empowerment Process

Empowerment means having a positive and accurate sense of self and being able to take action based on that sense of self. The process of empowerment includes four steps:

1. It begins with identifying crucial issues or questions. Name your questions and concerns about multicultural education.

2. Next pass the questions "...back and forth with friends and colleagues so that they can be shared, expanded, analyzed, and criticized through open communication" (York 1988, 7).

3. Combine the heightened awareness and understanding with action. Critical thinking about these issues with others gives you the support and encouragement that are needed to take informed action.

4. Reflect on your actions by evaluating the experience. Identify the positive and negative consequences and any new obstacles that should be considered.

Facilitating Empowerment

When I was a program director, I learned I just couldn't buy a book for each of the staff, require them to read it, and expect them to incorporate multicultural education into the curriculum by the end of the year. Teachers need structure to encourage and facilitate the empowerment process. This includes regularly scheduled blocks of time to meet with others committed

to multicultural education. Meetings can be held weekly, biweekly, or monthly depending on the program schedule. Staff also need a place to meet that is away from children and interruptions, perhaps during naptime or in the evenings. Finally, they need a framework to support the empowerment process. Two models provide the necessary structure for this purpose.

A support group. The framework to achieve empowerment may be very loose so that the regular meetings are like a support group. Louise Derman-Sparks recommends forming support groups as the first step in implementing anti-bias curriculum. In a support group, teachers help each other with the struggles and questions of learning how to provide an anti-bias environment for children. Activities of a support group might include observing children and then coming back to share observations. Choosing a book to read and discuss together is another possibility. Teachers can also brainstorm activity ideas and share resources. A support-group approach like this works well when you and your coworkers have been together for a long time and are already sensitive to your own prejudices.

An educational support group. Your program may experience high staff turnover. You may not be aware of how prejudice and bias affect your life or the lives of the children in your classroom. If this is the case, a support group that includes educational sessions can empower while at the same time increase awareness and understanding of the critical issues involved in implementing multicultural education. Administrators may want to bring in trainers and local experts to lead these sessions. Another option is to follow Carol Morgaine's model for working through bias and oppression.

Carol Morgaine's Progression: Critical Theory of Self Formation

Carol Morgaine's theory provides a tool to empower staff; it helps you and your coworkers understand how you are systematically oppressed by dominant societal forces. Morgaine describes her model as providing participants with ". . . an interactive-educational process . . . which facilitates an understanding of the interaction between an individual's personality development and the influences of society" (Morgaine 1988, 162). This model uses the techniques of empowering education to take participants through a sequence of topics that include authenticity, power, shame, defenses, addictions, prejudice, and oppression.

Using the Model with Staff

While Morgaine's model is very process oriented, it also provides a structure for personal consciousness raising. I have used it with early childhood teachers and find that it does indeed help teachers liberate themselves by encouraging them to examine personal experiences and become aware of society's values and messages. It awakens each staff person to the personal issues that underlie multicultural education. After going through the process, staff easily connect their caregiving practices, learning activities, curriculum themes, and program policies to issues such as authenticity, power, and shame.

A short-term educational support group could work through the model in seven weekly or monthly sessions, with each session focusing on a different topic. The University of Minnesota Child Care Center chose to spend nearly a year (13 sessions) on multicultural education. They began with a four-hour workshop that was held on a day when the center was closed. The rest of the sessions were held once a month in the evenings.

Each individual session can be two to three hours long and include a variety of learning experiences such as journaling, small group discussions, mini-lectures, and films.

Seven-Week Educational Support Group
Using the Morgaine Progression

Session 1:   Authenticity
Session 2:   Power
Session 3:   Shame
Session 4:   Defenses
Session 5:   Addictions
Session 6:   Prejudice
Session 7:   Oppression

University of Minnesota Child Care Center Inservice
Schedule Using the Morgaine Progression

Session 1:   Introduction and Authenticity
Session 2:   Power
Session 3:   Defenses
Session 4:   Addictions
Session 5:   Classism
Session 6:   Racism
Session 7:   Sexism
Session 9:   Homophobia
Session 10:   Ageism
Session 11:   Handicappism
Session 12:   Oppression
Session 13:   Review and Looking Ahead

Morgaine's Critical Theory

The following is a brief outline of the main elements of Morgaine's Theoretical Model. They are listed in sequence, as life experiences associated with each element build on one another to form our adult selves.

Life experience describes the negative life experiences that are often a part of growing up in our society. Children experience a lack of authenticity when parents ridicule them for who they are and praise them for being who the parents want them to be. Children must then put on a mask or a front and try to behave in ways that parents will accept, rather than acting in a way that fits their true selves. Read the descriptions under the life experience column and think about how that particular topic has influenced the formation of who you are as a person.

Resolution refers to the positive attitudes and abilities that grow out of personal reflection. As a result of questioning myself and reflecting on my life experiences, I come to know myself in new ways. I reformulate my opinion of myself. I am authentic when I know myself inside and out, accept myself for who I am, and can act on my own behalf. An authentic person speaks from an inner core rather than saying things to please others. An authentic person acts on an inner knowing of what is right and true. Compare yourself to the characteristics described in the resolution column. What do you need in order to gain that attitude or skill?

Questions to Ask suggests a central question that you can ask yourself to begin the process of reflecting back on how you have been molded and formed into the person you are today.

Steps to Implementing Multicultural Education in the Classroom

Remembering that it is easier to change things than people, begin implementing multicultural curriculum by taking all stereotypic materials out of your classroom. Don't throw away inappropriate books or bulletin boards, because they can be used to teach the concepts of real and unreal, or fair and unfair, later on.

Next, gather materials to make your own visual displays, bulletin boards, and learning games. As part of this step, collect photos, greeting cards, posters, and supplies to make visual displays and bulletin boards that reflect diversity. Gradually add these materials to the room. Take note of how the children and parents respond.

The third step requires purchasing materials and rearranging the environment into interest areas that support making choices. Interest areas will

Morgaine's Progression: A Model of Self Formation

Element	Life Experience	Resolution	Questions to Ask
Authenticity	Become who others want me to be. Live as an impostor.	Be who and what I am. Accept and affirm my uniqueness.	Who am I?
Power	Believe power is limited; I have it or I don't. Subordinate or dominate. Others get you to change by using manipulation, comparison, threats, and bribes.	Act out of personal power that comes from being authentic. Combine personal power with others to reach compromises.	How has power been used on me?
Shame	Feel inferior, defective, inadequate, unworthy. Self blame. As a result of power and loss of authenticity, feel the need to hide. Believe I will be abandoned if people see who I really am.	Know the source of my shame and affirm myself by giving myself positive messages.	How has shame affected my self concept?
Defenses	Use self-defeating behavior to protect myself from past and anticipated shame: denial minimizing, controlling, dualistic thinking, perfectionism, martyrdom, blaming, overgeneralizing, silence.	Walls come down. I am able to clearly and respectfully name my feelings, wants, and needs.	How has shame affected my behavior with others?

Used with permission of the author, Carol Morgaine, *A Critical Theory of Self Formation*, a thesis submitted to the graduate school of the University of Minnesota, Minneapolis, 1990.

Element	Life Experience	Resolution	Questions to Ask
Addictions	Groups of people develop characteristics and patterns that don't allow individuals to be authentic. Groups use power and deception to control individual's behavior. Defenses become systemized. Characterized by poor boundaries, no-talk rules, claim to know truth, denial.	Identify unhealthy group dynamics. Become aware of how addictive behavior is present in my family, work setting, schools, institutions, society.	What characteristics of addictive systems are present in my family? My work place?
Prejudice	Use illogical, protective, dualistic, compulsive beliefs of addictive system. Judging people on outer characteristics. Feel superior by thinking and acting like others are inferior. Need and force everyone to be the same in order to feel safe.	Become aware of classism, racism, sexism, ageism, handicappism, homophobia. Learn to affirm and value diversity.	How have I experienced -isms in my life? When did I first become aware of -isms?
Oppression	Use systems to re-enact how power was used on me. Prejudiced thinking justifies behavior. Society as an addictive system uses power to keep people in their place in order to protect a few. Results in feeling of rage, shame, frustration, hopelessness.	Become aware of institutionalized -isms. Gain an attitude of shared wealth, shared societal resources, societal benefits. Take a stand against injustice. Work to change oppressive structures—can't have moral end without moral means.	In what relationships do I oppress? In what situations have I been oppressed?

allow children to notice the differences in types of toys and play, and freely explore materials.

Once your classroom has been transformed, you can develop and incorporate multicultural education into the curriculum. This fourth step includes developing small and large group activities, creating alternative celebrations and rituals, and planning field trips and classroom visitors. Using multicultural learning materials and implementing multicultural activities will give you experience in talking with children about multicultural topics in structured settings.

The fifth step involves using daily events and experiences as opportunities to talk with children informally about multicultural concepts, experiences, and ideas. This includes bringing up issues with children or following up on issues or questions they raise during casual interactions such as arrival, departure, mealtimes, naptime, and free play.

The sixth step is more difficult. Now you confront children with their biased remarks and behavior as it occurs in the classroom. Hopefully by now you feel comfortable enough to answer a child's pointed question like, "Why does that man have ugly hair?" These are the most difficult situations for teachers to deal with because they catch us off guard. Feeling like you are on the spot, you try not to offend anyone or hurt their feelings.

The seventh and final step in implementing multicultural education is to incorporate an anti-bias component into the curriculum. This is achieved by adding cooperative learning experiences and opportunities for decision-making and group problem solving. As a teacher, you help the children to become aware of unfair situations and help them figure out ways to take action to confront or change them. Finally, the curriculum content is extended beyond culture and racism to include other discriminatory practices such as sexism, ageism, and homophobia.

Steps to Implement Multicultural Education

1. Remove stereotypic materials from the classroom.
2. Gather up existing multicultural materials and Make multicultural visual displays and teacher-made activities.
3. Purchase multicultural materials and rearrange the classroom environment.
4. Develop and implement small and large-group multicultural activities.
5. Use daily events to talk with children about concepts related to multicultural education.
6. Confront children on their biased remarks and behavior as it occurs in the classroom.
7. Expand content to address issues of bias like sexism, classism, ageism, handicappism, and homophobia.

Integrating Multicultural Education into the Entire Program

Multicultural education can involve parents and everyone who works in the early childhood center: administrators, support staff, and even cooks. Everyone, regardless of role or job title, has the opportunity to influence children by either perpetuating stereotypes and prejudiced behavior or by counteracting stereotypes and modeling respect and acceptance of diversity. Let's look at how each can participate in multicultural education.

Administrators

Administrators have the authority to initiate and sustain the movement toward adopting multicultural education. Begin the process by bringing staff together to discuss the current situation, raise issues, generate questions, and discuss possibilities. Support the process by making sure that staff are given a regularly scheduled time to meet and are provided with ongoing staff development experiences. Bring in resource people from the community and local experts to lead inservices and provide consultation. As an administrator, it is your responsibility to review the budget and allocate money for purchasing materials and supplies. Plan for long-term change by making the multicultural project a line item in the budget. If this is not possible, consider creating an annual fund raiser or writing a grant to generate funds to support the project. Set the direction by revising the program's mission statement, philosophy statement, and goals to include the multicultural emphasis and nondiscriminatory practices. Specific goals and objectives for the multicultural curriculum can be developed cooperatively by staff and parents. Enrollment forms and intake interviews can be revised to show sensitivity to and interest in each family's lifestyle. Finally, enrollment procedures, hiring procedures, and parent involvement practices must be reviewed for discrimination and tokenism.

Support Staff

Usually early childhood programs have a secretary, bookkeeper, or an administrative assistant. Often the person filling this role has the first contact with families and the community. It is important that the support staff recognize and support the multicultural project. Language used over the phone or in person must not be discriminatory or derogatory. Support staff can also assist the project by reviewing forms and center communication for biased language. This includes any community notices or announcements posted in the center. Depending on the clientele, some of the materials or forms may need to be translated into other languages. If the entry way and hallways are decorated with seasonal or holiday items, be sure that all displays are free of stereotypes and avoid overemphasizing Euro-American holidays and Christian celebrations.

Cooks

The cook can participate in the process by reviewing the food program and incorporating ethnic recipes into the regular snack and meal rotation. The cook can meet with parents interested in modifying the food program and request recipes from the families enrolled at the center. Make a point of including foods and recipes that children actually eat at home rather than gathering recipes of ethnic or exotic foods from cookbooks. Gradually begin to incorporate the foods and recipes into the daily menu. Make a recipe book and distribute it to all of the families or sell it as a fund raiser for multicultural materials. As a cook, be sensitive to seasonal and cultural celebrations that the teachers observe in their classrooms. When teachers and cooks work together, the daily snack or meal can complement the classroom activities.

Parents

Involve parents in the process from the beginning. Schedule a parent meeting during the initial stages of the project to share with them the current situation, staff questions and concerns, and the possibilities for the future. Ask parents to voice their questions and concerns, as well as support and encouragement. Keep parents informed throughout the process with a column in your program's monthly newsletter. Ask for parents' assistance in gathering materials and making learning games. Parents can share their family customs, rituals, and recipes with their child's class. Offer an ongoing support group or a parent education class that corresponds with the multicultural curriculum taking shape in the classroom. *Process Parenting*, *Parenting with a Global Perspective*, and *Parenting for Peace and Justice* are examples of parent education curriculum that could be used with parents of young children. Ensure the ongoing participation of parents by setting up a parent advisory board to work with you in developing and implementing a multicultural curriculum.

Problems with Change

Adopting or improving multicultural education changes an early childhood program. As such, efforts to add multicultural education are susceptible to all of the forces that can work against change. Become aware of these influences at the beginning so that you can watch for them and deal with them as they arise.

One Change Causes More Change

Early childhood programs are like machines, made up of many different parts that work together to keep the program in operation. What happens to one segment of the program affects the entire program. Don't assume you work alone or can make changes in one classroom without affecting—and perhaps upsetting—everyone else.

Resistance to Change

By our human nature we resist change. Even when things are going well and a program appears healthy, the staff may resist change. If you have been around for a long time, you may want things to stay the way they have always been. Beginning the process of implementing multicultural education with staff empowerment can reduce the natural tendency to avoid change.

Staff Turnover

Have you ever worked in a program that began to make changes and then something happened to prevent those changes from taking place? Staff turnover often puts a halt to good changes. A teacher might take initiative and make a lot of creative multicultural teaching materials. When that key person leaves, however, the program suffers a major setback. The creative teaching materials either go out the door with the teacher who leaves or they aren't used because the new teachers aren't sure how to use them. Your program can lose the energy and drive for implementing a multicultural component because of turnover.

Staff Conflict

You and your coworkers may not know very much about multicultural education. Some staff members may have distorted, inaccurate ideas about what is appropriate to teach young children. This can result in staff members disagreeing about what should be taught. When this happens, staff need a skilled leader to facilitate a compromise and resolve the conflict.

Mistakes

Sometimes we make mistakes in the process of making changes, mistakes that cause us to give up. At one child care center, I informed the parents of the new multicultural program with a letter and a detailed questionnaire. Many parents became angry over this unannounced letter and survey. They felt threatened and scared that big changes were on the way and that the center would never be the same. They had many questions and wanted them answered now, this minute. Ooops! Dealing with angry parents is scary for even the most seasoned teacher or director, and for a while I wished I had never initiated the project.

Outside Influences

Early childhood programs don't operate in a vacuum. Sometimes outside forces have a negative impact on the change process.

Current social and political policies. Social and political influences affect educational and human service programs. In the 1970s, when politics were more liberal, teachers had more freedom and were encouraged to try alternative education methods and models. The seventies were also a time of heightened awareness of discrimination. The conservatism of the 1980s and '90s brought the emphasis in education to the "basics" and preparing children for future success. Many of the programs were dropped, and curriculum materials developed during the seventies are no longer in print.

Fortunately, NAEYC's Center Accreditation Project and the anti-bias curriculum out of Pacific Oaks College have helped renew interest in multicultural and anti-bias education.

Money problems. Funding cuts can mean spending freezes, the loss of planning time, reduction of staff inservices, and the lay-off of staff. When programs are cut back, morale is low, and all a program can do is maintain its daily functions and raise staff trust. This is not a time to ask staff to put out extra effort for program development. Put any new or extra projects on hold and get through the current crisis. Revive the multicultural education project when the program has stabilized.

Conclusion

Implementing multicultural education is a difficult and often over-whelming task. Its core issues of discrimination, judgmental attitudes, feelings of superiority, humiliation and shame, and power and oppression tug at our hearts. By its nature, multicultural education forces staff members to reexamine values, beliefs, and lifestyles. This pushes us to go back to our own roots and reflect on (and perhaps see for the first time) biased and prejudiced attitudes and behavior in our parents, grandparents, and ancestors before them. Self-examination calls us to be open, honest, persistent, and courageous.

Multicultural education includes working on the classroom, the activities, the interaction between children and adults, the food service program, the enrollment forms and procedures, the budget, and parent involvement. The whole program and every staff member must become involved. Refer to this chapter when you need a boost, when you are trying to understand the change process, when you are designing teacher inservice sessions, and when you are ready to take the next step.

Questions to Ponder

1. How would you describe multicultural education?
2. What are your goals for multicultural education?
3. What knowledge, talents, and strengths do you bring to this project?
4. What information would you like to gain and what skills do you need to develop in order to implement a multicultural curriculum?
5. With whom can you share this project? Who will support you?
6. How do you normally deal with change?

Resources and References

Arnold, Rick, and Bev Burke. *A Popular Education Handbook*. Toronto: CUSO/Ontario Institute for Studies in Education, 1983.

Auvine, Brian, Betty Densmore, Mary Extrom, Scott Poole, Michel Shanklin. *A Manual For Group Facilitators*. Madison, WI: The Center For Conflict Resolution, 1977.

Baker, Gwendolyn C. *Planning and Organizing for Multicultural Instruction*. Reading, PA: Addison-Wesley, 1983.

Coover, Virginia, Ellen Deacon, Charles Esser, and Christopher Moore. *Resource Manual For A Living Revolution*. Philadelphia: New Society Publishers, 1977.

Cutting, Beth, and Ann Lovrien. *Parenting With A Global Perspective*.St. Paul: Minnesota State Department of Education, 1986.

Freire, Paulo. *Pedagogy of the Oppressed*. New York: Continuum, 1970.

McGinnis, Kathleen and James. *Parenting for Peace and Justice*. Maryknoll, NY: Orbis, 1981.

Miller, Alice. *For Your Own Good*. New York: Farrar, Straus, Giroux, 1983.

Morgaine, Carol. *A Critical Theory of Self Formation*. a Master's thesis University of Minnesota, Minneapolis, MN: 1990.

Prescott, Elizabeth. "The Physical Setting in Day Care," *Making Day Care Better*. Edited by James T. Greenman and Robert W. Fuqua. New York: Teachers College Press, 1984.

York, Stacey L. *Hearing Parent Themes: A Step Toward Liberating Parent Education*. Master's thesis, Pacific Oaks College, Pasadena, CA, 1988.

CHAPTER 4

‫⊐⊏⊐⊏⊐⊏⊐⊏⊐⊏⊐⊏⊐⊏⊐⊏⊐⊏⊐⊏⊐⊏⊐⊏⊐⊏⊐⊏‬

Teaching Through the Classroom Environment

The quickest and easiest way to add or improve multicultural education is to improve the classroom—it's easier to change things than it is to change people (Prescott 1984). Implementing multicultural education calls for changing the classroom environment as well as the people who teach in it. Moving furniture around, buying new toys and books, and making visual displays is simpler and personally less threatening than examining our biases and changing the way we teach or treat children.

Working on the classroom first allows you to roll up your sleeves and dig in right away. This is important because we teachers are active, practical people who would much rather be doing something than sitting around talking about far-off ideas. So jump into multicultural education and get started with the classroom.

A Good Place To Start

At some level, most early childhood teachers already know that starting with the room arrangement is a good idea. Ask a teacher what she does for multicultural education. Most often the answer is: "The center has a set of multi-ethnic dolls that we rotate from room to room. Our director bought each classroom a few books and a poster. I put the things out but now I don't know what to do next." Although many programs and teachers begin in the right place, they don't go far enough to realize their goals. Because they aren't sure the few materials are making an impact on the children and they don't have any more money in the equipment budget, they stop. Not knowing what else to do, they become stuck and bewildered.

This chapter will help you go beyond buying a few dolls and posters. It includes many ideas for teaching through interest areas, a criteria to follow in reviewing books and materials for stereotypes, suggestions for making your own visual displays, and a long list of sources for multicultural materials. Let's begin with a brief discussion about how room arrangement relates to program goals and the importance of classrooms in facilitating developmentally appropriate education for young children.

Classrooms Affect Behavior, Attitudes, and Learning

Classroom environments give children and parents strong messages. The arrangement of equipment and the display of materials affects children's behavior, learning, and attitudes. Open classrooms with toy shelves flush against the walls encourage running and rough-housing. Piling different kinds of toys onto one set of shelves gives children the message that it's acceptable to combine toys and to replace them in any order. Creating separate play areas and labeling the areas and shelves help children learn identification, matching, and classification concepts (Dodge 1978).

Convey Acceptance of Diversity

The classroom conveys attitudes to the children and parents by what is included in the room and what is left out. Omissions can be just as destructive as stereotypes and inaccurate information. Leaving multicultural education out of the curriculum gives children and families the message that it isn't important: "You don't need to know this . . . This doesn't relate to your life . . . You are too young to learn about this." It is our job as early childhood

teachers to make sure that the classroom includes all kinds of people doing all sorts of things and living out their daily lives in many different ways. This may be through visual images such as pictures or representations in the form of artwork and objects from daily life. Remember that displaying just one or two pictures is tokenism. It gives children the message, "Yes, these people are out there in the world somewhere, but you don't have to take them seriously."

Promote Active Learning Through Play

Physical space and room arrangement influence the length of activities, the number of choices available to children at any one time, and the presentation of activities. By looking at a classroom, you can tell what and how children are taught. Room arrangement silently communicates a program's philosophy toward early childhood education. It says, "This is how we believe children learn, and this is what we want children to learn." There are three basic principles underlying the organization and arrangement of a good early childhood classroom that supports multicultural education:

1. Children learn through play and should spend much of their day engaged in free-choice play where they can move independently about the room, make choices regarding their activities, and freely explore the people and materials that interest them.

2. Toys, books, and other learning materials should be organized into at least five clearly defined interest areas and displayed neatly on low, open shelves so that children can tell what their choices are and select their materials without adult assistance.

3. As teachers, we present the curriculum through the room arrangement by selecting materials, arranging materials on the shelves, rotating materials regularly, and changing the visual displays.

**Steps for Adding Multicultural Materials
and Creating New Visual Displays**

1. Arrange the room into at least five clearly defined interest areas.

2. Divide up the space and segregate the interest areas with barriers such as shelf units, couches, cubbies, and other large pieces of equipment.

3. Take toys out of their original containers and display them on shelves in "neutral" plastic containers, dish tubs, trays, or baskets.

4. Remove all stereotypic materials from the classroom.

5. Label the toys and shelves with pictures and words. Include labels in the children's native languages (Williams and DeGaetano, 1985)

Guidelines for Selecting Multicultural Materials

Begin implementing multicultural education in your classroom by removing stereotypic materials. You may be unsure of what is stereotypic and nonstereotypic. Fortunately, many guidelines are available for selecting multicultural books and classroom materials that will help you evaluate books and materials. Once the room is free of biased materials, use the criteria to help you select materials to purchase. The checklist on the following pages, developed by Bonnie Neugebauer, will help you get started.

Interest Centers

Children learn more through free-choice play than group times and structured activities. Interest centers organize children's free play and provide them with many choices. Through these areas children engage in open-ended activities that have few set rules and procedures. In addition, these areas are flexible and always changing to fit the children's interests and abilities or the curriculum theme.

Begin introducing multicultural curriculum by adding materials that reflect the culture of your children and the local community. Later, add a variety of materials and objects to represent diversity in the world and the many ways people live out their daily lives. You can also teach through the interest centers by adding materials to each area that support the unit theme.

What Are We Really Saying to Children?
Criteria for the Selection of Books and Materials

by Bonnie Neugebauer

Children receive messages from myriad sources within the context of the early childhood environment. We must be conscious of the messages which come through our words and actions and silences, and we must evaluate the messages inherent in the materials we provide. Only when we are deliberately selecting and evaluating can we hope that the messages children receive while in our care are consistent with the philosophy and goals of our programs.

For a quick and easy way to evaluate your entire library and classroom, ask parents and other staff to take a few books/materials and an equal number of photocopies of this checklist to review on their own.

Look for the Messages in Children's Books

Evaluate the Characters

Yes   No

❑   ❑   Do the characters in the story have personalities like real people?
❑   ❑   Do they seem authentic in the way they act and react?
❑   ❑   Do they speak in a style and language that fits their situation?
❑   ❑   Are they real people with strengths and weaknesses rather than stereotypes?
❑   ❑   Are characters allowed to learn and grow?
❑   ❑   Is their lifestyle represented fairly and respectfully?

Evaluate the Situation

❑   ❑   Do the characters have power over their own lives?
❑   ❑   Do they resolve their own problems and reap their own rewards?
❑   ❑   Are human qualities emphasized?

Evaluate the Illustrations

❑   ❑   Do the illustrations depict ethnic, age, cultural, economic, ability, and sexual differences respectfully? (Illustrations can be humorous, but they must fit the context of the story line and be consistent in portrayal.)
❑   ❑   Do the illustrations and the text work well together to communicate the story?
❑   ❑   Is the style of illustration appropriate to the story?

Evaluate the Messages

Yes No

❑   ❑   Do the messages conveyed, both directly and indirectly, respectfully and accurately portray the human condition?

❑   ❑   Are there hidden messages which are demeaning in any way or which reinforce stereotypes?

Evaluate the Author/Illustrator's Credibility

❑   ❑   Does the author/illustrator's background and training prepare her or him to present this story? (Do not disregard, but do consider carefully, stories about women written by men, stories about people with handicaps written by people without handicaps, stories about one ethnic group written by another.)

Consider Your Selection as a Whole

It is not possible for any one book to portray all that we want to say to children, so it is important to look at your whole library:

❑   ❑   Are there stories about the contemporary life of a given ethnic group as well as tales and legends?

❑   ❑   Do the cultures represented in your library at least cover (and optimally extend well beyond) those cultures represented by the families in your program?

❑   ❑   Are there books in which the disability or racial or economic difference is just part of the context for a story about people's lives, as well as books which focus on that particular difference?

Look for the Messages in Materials and Equipment

❑   ❑   Does this toy stereotype people by sex, race, age, family situation, physical, or intellectual skills?

❑   ❑   Does the selection of materials as a whole represent the diversity of humankind?

❑   ❑   How long will this toy hold a child's interest?

❑   ❑   Can it be adapted or used in different ways to change with different interests and ages of children?

❑   ❑   Can it be combined with other play materials to extend its possibilities?

❑   ❑   Is it safe, sturdy, appealing?

❑   ❑   Does the packaging of the toy reflect diversity? (If not, throw it away or use it for discussion, and write to the manufacturer.)

❑   ❑   Is the way in which children play with these materials consistent with your program's philosophy and goals?

Reprinted with permission from *Alike and Different: Exploring Our Humanity with Young Children* (ed) by Bonnie Neugebauer—a beginning book for teachers of young children. Exchange Press, PO Box 2890, Redmond, WA 98073.

Art Area

The art area gives children opportunities to explore various art materials and to express themselves. In early childhood education the emphasis is on the process of exploring different media, learning to use art materials, expressing feelings and a sense of self, and making representations of the world and one's experience in it. In a multicultural classroom the art materials must include colors, patterns, and textures from other cultures. Try adding origami paper for folding, rice paper for painting, and red clay for modeling. Collage materials could also be available such as magazines with pictures of people from different cultures, a file of pre-cut pictures, or fabric scraps of imported cloth. In addition, the art area should be stocked with skin-colored crayons, markers, paint, paper, collage materials, and playdough. Consider setting out hand mirrors so that children can look at themselves and notice their skin color and facial features before drawing pictures of themselves or other people. Include visual displays illustrating the artwork, color schemes, and visual patterns of other cultures.

Block Area

Blocks adapt well to a multicultural environment because they are the most versatile piece of equipment in an early childhood classroom. Through block play, children explore math, science, and spatial relations concepts. They also engage in fantasy play and make representations of the real world. In addition, the flexibility of blocks is characterized by the fact that children can play alone, side-by-side, or cooperatively with one another. If you add multicultural accessories and props to a full set of hardwood unit blocks, you will guide and expand children's play. Such props can include a variety of transportation toys such as trains, buses, double-decker buses, planes, jets, cars, horses and carts, ferries, barges, canoes, and sleds. Multi-ethnic, nonsexist wooden play figures as well as small dolls and paper dolls from other countries increase the variety of people. Lincoln Logs building blocks and raw materials such as cardboard, boxes, canvas, string, and masking tape encourage children to build their own buildings and houses. Try adding palm leaves, coconut branches, corn husks, pine branches, bark, pine needles, Popsicle (craft) sticks, stones and straw for creating roofs, houses, and fences. Display pictures of buildings from different parts of the world such as a pagoda, treehouse, adobe, hogan, thatched hut, log home, sod home, tent, earth sheltered home, apartment building, trailer, and hotel. Rubber, plastic, wooden, cloth, and carved-bone animals representing the jungle, tropical forest, desert, and forest will also enhance the children's play.

Music Area

The music area offers children a chance to experiment with and enjoy a variety of music. In this area, children listen to music, create their own music, compare and contrast sounds, move to sound, and learn about and play different instruments. Build up a broad selection of both vocal and instrumental music. Ask parents to make a cassette tape of the music their family and children enjoy at home. Use music from different cultures as background music during free play and naptime. Teach children songs with simple words and melodies from other cultures and teach them songs that encourage differences, acceptance, and cooperation. Add instruments such as kalimbas, maracas, Tibetan bells, gongs, gourds, metal and bongo drums, woven jute rattles, wooden flutes, brass bells, conch shells, castanets, wooden xylophones, and guitars to the set of traditional rhythm instruments. Many cultures use drums and drumming as their main instrument. Though expensive, a good drum provides a wonderful sound that can serve as the basic background instrument for many music activities.

Dramatic Play

In this interest area, children act out their everyday experiences, play out their perceptions of the world, try on adult roles, and explore relationships among people. Like the block area, the dramatic play area encourages cooperative play among children. Here, children come to a greater understanding of themselves and gain a sense of the lifestyles that are available to them. The dramatic play area, like other areas, must allow children to explore a variety of lifestyles, including family systems, economic class, and culture. In this context, children try on the roles of people of different ages, skills, and occupations. Add a full-length mirror, large plastic crates, hollow blocks, planks, and large pieces of fabric to the basic housekeeping equipment. This allows children to create a variety of homes, floor plans, or places to visit away from home. With older children, consider designing a two or three room dramatic play area that includes a living room and a bedroom along with the traditional kitchen. Rather than teaching a particular culture, the dramatic play props should emphasize the many ways of going about our daily lives such as kinds of food to eat, types of eating utensils, and ways of dressing. Begin with items children have in their homes and expand from there. Consider adding the following accessories and props to the dramatic play area:

Dolls: multi-ethnic dolls.

Food containers: tea boxes, tea tins, canned foods, cardboard food containers, plastic bottles, plastic play food. Stuff rice, flour, and potato bags with batting and sew them closed. Make cardboard or wooden slices of bread and stuff them into various bread bags.

Food storage containers: baskets, gourds, mesh bags, pottery.

Cooking utensils: tortilla presses, molenellos, tea balls, rolling pins, strainers, ladles, woks, steamers, food grinders, mortars and pestles, cutting boards, frying pans, kettles.

Eating utensils: silverware, wooden spoons, spatulas, graters, egg beaters, whisks, rice bowls, wooden bowls and plates, tin plates, plastic plates, teacups, chopsticks, tea pots, coffee pots.

Clothes: dresses, skirts, jackets, large pieces of fabric for clothing in squares, rectangles, and triangles. Pick out different patterns such as batik, tie-dyed, and madras prints. Include saris, kimonos, serapes, dashikis, kentes, grass skirts, woven vests, shawls, ponchos, tunics, kaffiya scarves. Include seasonal clothing like heavy coats, scarves, mittens, boots, and hats for winter.

Shoes: sandals, mukluks, clogs, moccasins, huaraches, getas, wooden shoes, boots, slippers, dress shoes.

Hats: berets, turbans, sombreros, straw hats, Chinese peoples' caps, baseball caps, felt hats, knit hats.

Beds: woven mats, futons, cots, mattress, blankets, hammocks.

Miscellaneous: placemats, vases, trivets, masks, bags, scarves and kerchiefs, sashes, coins, fans, hair combs and brushes, umbrellas, fishing nets, area rugs, baby carriers, and jewelry.

Manipulative Area (Table Toys)

In the manipulative area, children work alone and with friends to put together puzzles, play board games, and complete classification and sequencing activities. Through these purchased and home-made activities and games, children explore concepts of alike and different, whole-part relationships, one-to-one correspondence, and skills such as sequencing, visual discrimination, and recognizing symbols. This area can be enhanced with multi-ethnic, nonsexist puzzles available through many common toy catalogues. Sets of graduated items from other cultures such as wooden dolls or animals make fun sequencing games. Make your own activities such as sorting foreign coins, shells, dried beans, ethnic fabric squares, and other raw materials. Make lotto, classification, and matching games such as "Which One Is Different?" "Match Ups," "Mothers and Babies," and "Fair and Unfair" as presented in Chapter 5. Because of stereotypic packaging, make it a practice to take toys out of their original container and display them in plastic dish tubs or on trays.

Science Area

This area offers children an opportunity to examine the elements and properties of the natural world. It's a wonderful area for observing differences and learning the importance of respect and care for all living things. Multicultural activities might include a collection of rocks, semi-precious stones, and shells from different parts of the world. Terrariums and miniature indoor gardens model different types of soil, ground covering, and vegetation. The display might include a small cactus garden in sand, a planting of ferns in soil heavy with peat and sphagnum moss on the top, a bonsai display with smooth pebbles, a fish tank with plants that grow under the water, a Norfolk Island pine tree with bark chips, a dwarf citrus tree in sandy loam, a palm tree, a bamboo tree, or a tropical flowering ornamental like a hibiscus or azalea. Include pictures and photographs of gardens from around the world. Grow herbs that are used in cooking foreign foods in a sunny window. Cilantro, lemon grass, oregano, basil, mint, sage, sweet grass, and parsley are good choices. Add smells and scents from other cultures to the smelling jar kit. Create collections of different kinds of grains, beans, and soils. Examples of grains include wheat berries, rye berries, oats, millet, corn, couscous, barley, white rice, brown rice, red rice, and wild rice. A complete assortment of dried beans would include black-eyed peas, baby limas, black beans, adzuki, pinto, kidney, great northern, soybeans, and lentils. Look for bulk grains and beans at your local food co-op or health food store.

(Some teachers may choose not to use food as a teaching tool. This decision is based on personal values and each teacher must make her own choice.)

Sensory Table

Children are introduced to different textures and fluid media at the sensory table. They learn about comparing and measuring amounts and the characteristics of various materials, so vary the materials in the sensory table to correspond with the curriculum. Try to include textures and smells that represent not only the children in the class but other cultural groups as well. Many of the grains and dried beans listed under the science area can be purchased in large quantities to fill the sensory table. Other dry materials for the table include whole nuts in the shell, bark, dry leaves, coffee beans, soil, different kinds of flour, saw dust, raw cotton, raw wool, raw silk, and flax. When exploring liquids with the children, try adding a scent to the water. Small bottles of essential oils can be purchased at health food stores or international gift shops, and they come in various floral, wood, citrus, and herbal scents.

The sensory table can also be used for dramatic play. The addition of small people figures, transportation toys, twigs, rocks, and miniature plastic plants to a base of sand, soil, or water allows children to create environments that are unfamiliar as well as recreate environments that are common in their everyday lives (Williams and DeGaetano 1985). For example, children in northern Minnesota and parts of Kentucky may be very familiar with mines. They could play "mine" with wet sand, rocks, and a collection of small trucks, front-end loaders, shovels, and small people figures. Likewise, a high-rise construction site could be created with a layer of dirt, a crane, trucks, small building blocks, and play figures. A desert could be created with sand, rocks, and small desert animal figures. Other options include a dam, a beach with sand and shells, a river or lake, mountains, or a farm.

Book/Quiet Area

The quiet area provides children with a cozy, inviting place to look at books. Here children learn to care for and appreciate books; they also develop skills in turning pages, telling stories, sequencing events, recalling events, imaginative thinking, and listening. Begin by creating a soft and cozy setting. Large floor pillows and cushions in ethnic prints invite children to snuggle up with a friend and look at books. Large overstuffed chairs, mattresses, or loveseats encourage adults to gather a child on their lap for an individual storytime. Display books that emphasize diversity, ethnicity, different lifestyles, and cooperation. Include alphabet and counting books from other cultures. A cassette player and story tapes add to the interest area. Look for stories that include ethnic background music and narration by a person from that culture. You and your children can supplement your current library with homemade books. For instance, take pictures of the children and create your own books. Have the children make books about themselves and their families.

It can be very difficult to locate appropriate multicultural books for young children. The reference librarian at the local public library can order any book you request through its interlibrary loan system. Another option is to get to know a local bookseller. As you work with your local librarian and bookseller you will educate them on what it is that you need, and they'll begin contacting you when they come across new titles in their publishers catalogs. Louise Derman-Spark's *Anti-Bias Curriculum* contains an excellent ten-page listing of books for children that cover a variety of topics: individual and family identity, sex roles, people with disabilities, the effects of discrimination and the possibilities of activism. Use her resource list to guide you.

Visual Displays

Visual displays add the final touch to creating a multicultural classroom. Remember that we want children to notice and interact with the materials on the shelves and the displays on the table. We don't want them wandering around or flitting from area to area because they can't tell what their options are. The overuse of visual displays creates "visual noise" that distracts children from the materials. Rather than filling every inch of wall space with bulletin boards, pictures, and posters, try using these materials as if you were decorating a home environment. Use and create visual displays to match, reinforce, and expand the materials and learning that takes place in each of the interest centers. For example, display works of art in the art area, posters of buildings and environments in the block area, and pictures of people, families, and daily life scenes in the dramatic play area. Classroom entrance areas, parent sign-in tables, hallways, cubby areas, and bathrooms can become warmer, more welcoming spaces with the use of a few well-chosen and well-placed visual displays.

Emphasize Real Life

Creating an aesthetically pleasing environment that is also multicultural means avoiding the use of cartoon characters such as dolls in costumes, animal characters dressed in ethnic costumes, and stereotypic pictures of people in their traditional dress. Appropriate display materials include artwork and artifacts from existing cultures:

fabric	musical instruments
paintings	sculpture
beadwork	windsocks/windchimes
rugs	photos (magazine and purchased)
wall hangings	

Acquiring Visual Materials

It is time-consuming, difficult, and expensive to acquire a large selection of multicultural display materials for the classroom. Some educational catalogues carry modern, accurate teaching posters and picture sets. Large cities may offer resources at UNICEF gift shops, educational supply centers, Third World self-help craft shops, international and ethnic gift shops, museum gift shops, and alternative or women's bookstores (Derman-Sparks 1989). Don't overlook nationwide chain stores such as Pier 1 Imports.

Travels. Another way to acquire multicultural materials is to purchase materials when traveling on the continent or abroad. Ask friends who may

travel internationally to pick up materials for the classroom. I have a good friend with an early childhood background who travels to Japan and Europe regularly. Our center gave her $200 from the equipment budget to purchase children's books, toys, posters, and other interesting items she might find for our classrooms. She brought back wonderful things and was able to purchase them at a much lower cost than if we had purchased them here.

Photographs and Magazine Pictures. Making homemade materials and visual displays is perhaps the most viable way to create a multicultural classroom environment. Photographs from magazines provide pictures of people living out their daily lives in the present. It is common for teachers to maintain a picture file for curriculum units. Consider starting a multicultural picture file.

When enough photographs have been gathered they can be mounted and laminated. Display the photographs separately or create a collage on posterboard. Collages may focus on a specific theme such as boys and girls, babies, faces, grandparents, families, homes, or workers. Create a collage of pictures of people from a specific ethnic group. This type of collage is particularly useful because it shows the diversity and individuality within an ethnic group.

Not all magazines are useful sources of multicultural pictures. Thumbing through popular women's magazines like *Good Housekeeping*, *Family Circle*, and *Better Homes and Gardens* for appropriate photographs proves that people of color are excluded in mainstream media. Be careful, too, of *National Geographic*. It tends to highlight people in faraway places dressed in traditional costumes at special celebrations (Derman-Sparks 1989). Below is a list of magazines that tend to include useful photographs:

   regional magazines like *Sunset*, *Arizona Highways*
   airline magazines (especially the carriers that fly worldwide)
   department store magazine advertisements
   Sunday newspaper magazines like the *New York Times Magazine*
   CHILD
   Parents
   Parenting
   Working Mother
   People
   Life
   Ebony
   Essence
   Jet
   MS
   Faces (see the resource list)

Postcards and Greeting Cards. Postcards and greeting cards are also sources of pictures for visual displays and teaching materials. Hallmark greeting card stores are likely to carry traditional stereotypic cards like cartoon turkeys wearing an Indian headdress wishing you a Happy Thanksgiving. However, these cards can be useful in teaching what is untrue and unfair. Independent card shops may carry a greater selection of cards with wonderful color photographs and photographic postcards of people from all over the world.

Polaroid Camera. It can take a long time to develop a comprehensive picture file. Create visual displays as well as children's books by taking photos with a camera. Take the camera on home visits or loan it to families so they can take pictures of their family at home that can then be used in the classroom. Take the camera along on field trips. Take pictures of special visitors to the classroom. Also take pictures of the local neighborhood and community. A teacher at a rural early childhood program may want to take pictures of a local migrant child care program. A teacher at a suburban program could take pictures of children at a local inner city program. Of course, permission would need to be granted. But perhaps a relationship between the programs could develop as a result.

Classroom Resources

The following companies provide good materials for transforming your classroom. Write or call them for their catalog or for further information:

American Guidance Service (AGS), PO Box 99, Circle Pines, MN 55014. (800) 328-2560.
PEEK: Peabody Card and Picture Deck, I Am Amazing Program, multi-layered puzzles, sequencing cards.

Afro-American Publishing Company, 819 S. Wabash Avenue, Chicago, IL 60605. (312) 922-1147.
Multicultural materials including Colors Around Us study prints.

American Indian Resource Center, 6518 Miles Avenue, Huntington Park, CA 90255. (213) 583-1461.
Teaching materials, books.

Animal Town, P.O. Box 2002, Santa Barbara, CA 93120. (800) 445-8642.
Specializes in cooperative games and books on cooperative family activities.

Baby Poster, P.O. Box 4109, Department 2, Monticello, MN 55365.
Kodak baby and sequel posters.

Bilingual Educational Services, Inc., 2514 S. Grand Avenue, Los Angeles, CA 90007. (213) 749-6213.
Bilingual books, dictionaries, posters.

Center For Media Development, Inc., P.O. Box 51, Great Neck, NY 11021.
Talk About Picture Activity Cards.

Childcraft, 20 Kilmer Road, P.O. Box 3081, Edison, NJ 08818. (800) 631-5652.
Block play figures, plastic play food, pliable people, family puppets, multicultural baby dolls, multi-ethnic dolls, sound/listening games, male nurturing puzzles, birthday sequence puzzle, drums, nonsexist career puzzles, nonsexist community careers for flannel board.

Children's Book and Music Center, 2500 Santa Monica Blvd., Santa Monica, CA 90406. (800) 443-1856.
Large selection of children's books, records, audiocassettes, instruments.

Claudia's Caravan, P.O. Box 1582, Alameda, CA 94501. (415) 521-7871.
Large collection of multicultural teaching materials.

Cross Cultural Communication Centre (CCCC), 965 Bloor Street W. Toronto, Ontario, Canada M6H 1L7. (416) 530-4117.
Multicultural Early Childhood Education bibliography.

Council on Interracial Books for Children. 1841 Broadway, New York, NY 10023. (212) 757-5339.

Teacher-training materials, filmstrips, journal articles.

DLM Teaching Resources, P.O. Box 4000, One DLM Park, Allen, TX 75002. (800) 527-4747.

I Am Freedom's Child book and audiotape, Questions: beginning level picture cards, Basic Concept stories, oral language development posters, Body and Self Awareness Big Box.

Donnelly/Colt. P.O. Box 188, Hampton, CT 06247. (203) 455-9621.

"Thank You, Sister Rosa Parks" poster, "Children's Innocence" poster, postcards, earth flag.

Education Equity Concepts, 114 E. 32nd Street, New York, NY. (212) 725-1803.

Inclusive play people, play scenes lotto, curriculum.

Educational Materials, Inc., 6503 Salizar Street, San Diego, CA 92111. (619) 277-7007.

Multicultural baby dolls, bilingual materials, wooden face puzzles, children at play, indoors puzzles, children at play outdoors puzzles.

Faces: The Magazine About People, Cobblestone Publishing, 20 Grove Street, Peterborough, NH 03458. (603) 924-7209.

Photographs for visual displays.

A Gentle Wind, P.O. Box 3103, Albany, NY 12203. (518) 436-0391.

Children's musical and story cassette tapes.

Global Village Toys, 2210 Wilshire Blvd., Suite 262, Santa Monica, CA. (213) 459-5188.

Multicultural toys, teaching materials, children's books.

Gryphon House, P.O. Box 275, Mt. Rainier, MD 20712. (800) 638-0928.

Children's books, teacher's books.

Information Center on Children's Cultures, United States Committee for UNICEF, 331 E. 38th Street, New York, NY 10016. (212) 686-5522.

Information sheets, children's books, musical cassette tapes, posters, Lingo game.

Institute for Peace and Justice, 4144 Lindell, Room 122, St. Louis, MO 63108. (314) 533-4445.

Parenting and curriculum materials focusing on social justice issues.

Judy Instructo, 4325 Hiawatha Avenue S., Minneapolis, MN 55406. (612) 721-5761.

Community careers flannel board aids, Families Early Learning curriculum unit, Discussion picture puzzles, Martin Luther King and Giant Floor puzzles. See QUEES storyboards.

Lakeshore, 2695 E. Dominquez Street, P.O. Box 6261, Carson, CA 90749. (800) 421-5354.

Lambskins for infants, large shatterproof wall mirrors, plastic food, pretend television set, multi-ethnic dolls, flexible doll families, flexible career doll set, wooden stand-up wedge career figures, clay, Kids at Play Photo Puzzle Set, Multicultural Study Prints Library.

Multicultural Project for Communication and Education, Inc. 186 Lincoln Street, Boston, MA 02111.

Book: *Cultural Links: A Multicultural Resource Guide*

Music for Little People, P.O. Box 1460, Redway, CA 95560. (800) 346-4445.

Musical and story cassette tapes, videos, instruments.

Music Mobile, Inc., P.O. Box 6024, Albany, NY 12206. (518) 462-8714.

Musical cassette tapes: *Look To The People* and *Under One Sky*.

Nasco, 901 Janesville Avenue, Fort Atkinson, WI 53538. (414) 563-2446.

20th Century Black Personalities teaching posters, *Black Mother Goose* book, ethnic dolls, Our Community Helpers play people, wooden play figures, black baby doll, Mexican-American play food, human body parts flannel aids, Senses puzzle.

National Association for the Education of Young Children (NAEYC), 1834 Connecticut Avenue N.W., Washington, DC 20009. (800) 424-2460.

Teacher-training videos, teacher books, parent brochures, large full-color posters.

National Black Child Development Institute, 1463 Rhode Island Avenue N.W., Washington, DC 20005. (202) 387-1281.

Journal and guidelines for selection of materials and early childhood education in public schools.

National Museum of Natural History, Smithsonian Institution, Washington, DC 20560.

Free newsletter for teachers, information leaflets, photographs, posters.

New Song Library, P.O. Box 295, Northhampton, MA 01061. (413) 586-9485.

Lending library of social change music that includes songbooks, records, cassette tapes. Children's cassette tapes available for purchase.

Northern Sun Merchandising, 2916 E. Lake Street, Minneapolis, MN 55406. (612) 729-2001.

Hug-A-Planet inflatable earth balls, Fannie Lou Hammer, Malcolm X,

Winnie Mandela, Bishop Tutu, and Circle of Life posters.

Northland Poster Collective, 1613 E. Lake Street, Minneapolis MN 55407. (800) 627-3082.

Posters, T-shirts, books, calendars, postcards, music cassette tapes.

Peace Resource Project, P.O. Box 1122, Arcata, CA 95521. (707) 822-4229.

Posters, rubber stamps.

Petley Studios, P.O. Box 24098, Tempe, AZ 85282. (602) 437-3909.

Indian arts prints.

Society for Visual Education, Inc., 1345 Diversity Parkway, Chicago, IL 60614.

Multicultural videos, fimstrips, study prints.

Song Bank, Peck Slip Station, P.O. Box 933, New York, NY 10272. (212) 285-8716.

New York City Lullabies audio cassette and *Singing the City to Sleep* video.

Storylines, P.O. Box 7416, St. Paul, MN 55107. (612) 643-4321.

Storytelling resources including storykeeper puppet and folktale cassette tapes.

Syracuse Cultural Workers, Box 6367, Syracuse, NY 13217. (315) 474-1132.

Beautiful posters and notecards suitable for visual displays. Peace Calendar, Nelson Mandela, Babies, Madre Hijo, Martin Luther King, and Sticks and Stones posters.

Toys 'n Things Press, 450 N Syndicate Avenue, Suite 5, St. Paul, MN 55104. (800) 423-8309.

Books for teachers, curriculum books.

U.S. Commitee For UNICEF, 1 Children's Blvd., Ridgely, MD 21685. (800) 553-1200.

Children's puzzles, games, cookbook, book of games from around the world.

United Indians of All Tribes Foundation, Community Educational Services, Discovery Park, P.O. Box 99100, Seattle, WA 98199. (206) 285-4425.

Daybreak Star Preschool Activities Book and other Native American curriculum materials.

Women's Educational Equity Act Publishing Center, Education Development Center, 55 Chapel Street, Suite 200, Newton, MA 02160. (800) 225-3088.

Teacher-training materials, checklist for bias.

Questions to Ponder

1. How are your program's goals reflected in the classroom?
2. How are your own attitudes and values reflected in your classroom?
3. What groups of people and ways of life are missing from your classroom?
4. List five things you can do to eliminate stereotypes from your classroom.
5. List five things you can do to increase diversity in your classroom.
6. Plan a curriculum unit and list at least two items supporting the unit theme that could be added in each interest area.

Resources and References

Derman-Sparks, Louise. *Anti-Bias Curriculum: Tools for Empowering Young Children.* Washington DC: NAEYC, 1989.

Kendall, Frances E. *Diversity in the Classroom: A Multicultural Approach to the Education of Young Children.* New York: Teachers College Press, 1983.

McNeill, Earldene, Velma Schmidt, and Judy Allen. *Cultural Awareness for Young Children.* Dallas: The Learning Tree, 1981.

Neugebauer, Bonnie. "Where Do We Begin? Bringing the World into Your Classroom." *Alike and Different: Exploring Our Humanity with Young Children.* Edited by Bonnie Neugebauer. Redmond, WA: Exchange Press, 1987.

Ramsey, Patricia G. *Teaching and Learning in a Diverse World: Multicultural Education for Young Children.* New York: Teachers College Press, 1987.

Texas Department of Human Services. *Culture and Children.* Austin: Texas Department of Human Services, 1985.

Williams, Leslie R., and Yvonne DeGaetano. *Alerta: A Multicultural, Bilingual Approach To Teaching Young Children.* Menlo Park: Addison-Wesley, 1985.

CHAPTER 5

Activities for Teaching Children About Culture

Early childhood educators teach through planned activities as well as a prepared environment. These planned activities are then grouped together to form the curriculum. Curriculum planning requires decision-making. Early childhood teachers must ask themselves: What messages do I want to convey to young children? What information would be developmentally appropriate? How might I organize a multicultural curriculum?

This chapter will help you plan curriculum units and meet the needs of individual children through curriculum. It will also help you decide what is developmentally appropriate and what information should be saved for presentation when children are older. Most importantly, this chapter provides you with over 50 multicultural activities for use in your classroom.

Multicultural Themes

Unit themes are probably the most popular way to organize learning in early childhood programs. Themes provide a focus, a topic around which to plan and choose activities. Ideas for themes may come from the teacher and manifest concepts she believes children should learn. Themes may come from the children, too, representing things they are asking questions about and are interested in learning more about. Themes also come from the physical and social world. For example, you probably plan themes about winter during the winter season, and children learn about Valentine's Day in February (Derman-Sparks 1987).

Many common early childhood themes can be expanded to include multicultural values (and the activities in this book). The following themes support and provide opportunities to explore multicultural concepts:

I'm Me and I'm Special	Books
Boys and Girls	Places People Live
Friends	Toys and Games

Families	Transportation
Our Community	Clothes We Wear
Food We Eat	Alike and Different
Day and Night	Light and Dark
Feelings	Holidays and Celebrations
Five Senses	Heroes
Music	Weather
Folk Tales	Animals
Dance and Movement	Pets
Bodies	Colors

Patricia Ramsey shows in her book, *Teaching and Learning in a Diverse World*, how multicultural concepts can be incorporated into a curriculum unit on pets. For example, a multicultural approach to learning about pets could include the following activities and topics adapted from her book:

Pets deserve our kindness because they are living beings.

Pets enrich our lives.

Taking care of a pet is a serious responsibility.

We can work together and share the responsibility of caring for a pet.

A pet can love many people.

Some pets are alike.

There are many different kinds of pets.

Pets and people are special friends, even though they are very differ-ent from one another.

Pets have babies and they take care of them in their own way.

We can work together to keep pets safe and healthy in our community.

Avoid themes like "Children Around the World" or "Let's Visit Hawaii." They encourage activities that focus on countries, artifacts, traditional clothing, and ceremonies. They teach children to be tourists (outsiders visiting an unknown culture that is totally irrelevant to their daily life). This method of curriculum planning teaches children trivia, ignores that people of other cultures really exist today and live normal everyday lives, and does nothing to build a foundation for living in a multicultural world. Children learn about the culture for a week, two weeks, or a month and then they move on to unit themes like the circus or dinosaurs. And the culture they just studied may not be talked about for the rest of the year.

Planning Multicultural Curriculum

Whether planning curriculum alone or with a teaching team, you'll want to consider all of the elements of an early childhood classroom. The follow-

ing curriculum planning form will help you consider such details as theme and concepts, important dates, parent newsletter articles, field trips, bulletin boards, cooking projects, and the room arrangement. It will give you a broad framework of the unit plan, be it a two-week time period or a month. Each team member can then take a copy of the general plan and use it to write up specific activities for free play and group time.

Using the Curriculum Planning Form

Theme. Decide on the theme and the length of time the class will spend on that unit. Select a theme from the list in this chapter or use one of your own.

Basic Concepts. Write down the basic concepts and ideas to which the children will be exposed through the activities offered in this unit. Remember that the early childhood years are not the time to emphasize learning facts and information. Use the theme to expose children to new experiences and invite them to explore new materials.

Special Dates. Go through the calendar and write down any special dates that take place during the time the class will be focusing on this particular unit. Also include children's birthdays if you celebrate them in your program. The calendar in Chapter 6 is a good source for dates.

Curriculum Planning Form

Theme: _____ **Weeks/Month:** _____

Basic Concepts:

_____

Special Dates:

Field Trips/Visitors:

Cooking Activities/Snacks:

Visual Displays:

Parent Newsletter:

_____

Classroom Environment

Book Area:

Art Area:

Block Area:

Small Muscle/Manipulative Area:

Dramatic Play Area:

Music/Movement Area:

Sand/Water Table:

Science Table:

Playground/Gym:

Field Trips/Visitors. Try to take one field trip each month. If you live in an area with harsh winters, substitute a field trip with a special visitor. Use the form to list places you might take the children or visitors you might invite into the classroom to emphasize the curriculum theme.

Cooking Activities/Snack. Some programs offer cooking as a weekly activity. These experiences are fun for children if they can actively participate in the preparation and cooking of food. Plan cooking experiences that support the unit theme. Plan a few special snacks or meals to go along with the theme if the center has a food service program. Remember, parents are a good source for recipes.

Visual Displays. Often teachers change the bulletin boards to go along with the curriculum theme. Bulletin boards can be important teaching tools. Think of displays that support the concepts you are trying to teach the children. Remember to include visual displays that show a variety of people in everyday situations. Use photographs and homemade displays as often as possible. Try to avoid cartoon figures that may be stereotypical and serve no purpose other than decoration.

Parent Newsletter. Most programs have some form of written communication with parents, be it a monthly classroom newsletter or an all-program newsletter. Write an article on the current theme and how you incorporate multicultural concepts and activities into the daily activities. Use this section to list ideas for newsletter articles and other information such as requests for materials, reports on a field trip or visitor, and sharing recipes.

Classroom Environment. The next section of the planning form lists the interest areas or learning centers often found in early childhood classrooms. Rotate and add materials that support the theme for each of the interest areas. In addition, use the curriculum planning form to delegate staff responsibilities for setting up or rearranging interest areas to go along with the theme. For example, one person may be responsible for returning and checking out new library books. Another person takes the art area and changes the colors of the paint and construction paper and makes new playdough.

Individualized Planning

Multicultural education includes accepting and respecting each child as an individual. It means recognizing what each child values and holds dear, and then building those things into the daily life of the early childhood program. New teachers often teach to their class as a group and are overwhelmed by the thought of considering and planning for individual children. Experienced teachers who have become comfortable and confident in their curriculum planning can take their skills one step farther by designing curriculum based on individual children's developmental abilities and interests. The curriculum that results from this practice is both child-centered and emergent: it comes from the child. It is naturally respectful and mindful of multicultural values because it takes each child's culture into account from the beginning.

The following individualized planning form helps you focus on each individual child in your class. It is written for a teaching team to complete together as a group. This activity can also be done by individual teachers who work alone with their own class.

Planning Multicultural Activities

As adults, we may think of countries, governments, languages, and customs when we hear the term, multicultural education. We remember our own experience of learning geography, making relief maps, and writing our first big report on the country of our choice. These are appropriate activities for elementary, junior high, and high school, but because of their cognitive development, young children are not ready to learn "facts" about different cultures, and they are easily confused by events that happened long ago or that occur in faraway places. As a result, teachers should avoid focusing on:

> names of countries
> locations of countries
> national flags
> historical events
> the concept of city, state, and nation
> revolutions and wars
> past presidents and rulers

In addition, young children may not believe that people from other cultures are real, or they may believe that they lived long ago and are no longer living in the world today. Activities that portray characteristics of other cultures as eccentric encourage children to believe in stereotypes. Young children may not recognize real people from other cultures when they see them on the street. They may say, "No, that's not an Indian. Indians wear feathers and ride horses." "No, she's not Japanese. She doesn't have a kimono or those funny shoes on." Teachers of young children should limit the amount of multicultural activities planned around these topics:

> foreign foods
> traditional costumes
> holidays and celebrations
> cultural artifacts

As early childhood educators, we know that children learn best when they are actively exploring materials, experiencing the world with their whole bodies and all of their senses, and interacting with a variety of people. Appropriate multicultural curriculum is no different from good curriculum. What we need to do is use a new perspective to examine existing activities and use good early childhood practices to deal with new issues (Derman-Sparks 1987).

Rather than simplifying elementary school activities and social studies lessons, try adapting proven early childhood activities. Avoid using worksheets, coloring pages, and craft projects. Go through your own activity files and curriculum books. As you review the activities you currently use every day in the classroom, think about how they might be modified to teach multicultural concepts.

The activities presented in this section provide many examples of how to use basic early childhood activities to emphasize multicultural concepts. The activities include creative arts, language arts, dramatic play, cognitive games, and group experiences.

Multicultural Concepts Young Children Can Understand

Appropriate multicultural activities for young children focus on things children are interested in and the concepts they are struggling to understand. Build your multicultural curriculum around activities that focus on these concepts:

Everyone is worthy.
Everyone is lovable and capable.
Everyone is equal.
Everyone deserves respect.
Everyone is important.
Everyone has feelings.
People are similar.
People are different.
Some physical attributes stay the same.
Some physical attributes change.
It is important to try new experiences.
We can learn about the daily life of
    people we know.
Culture comes from parents and
    family.
There are different kinds of families.
Families live in different ways.

Individualized Planning Form

1. Write the name of each child in your class on a piece of paper. Fold each slip of paper and place it in a paper bag. Mix up the slips and then draw four slips.
2. Write the names of the children selected on a blackboard or large sheets of easel paper.
3. Collect information on each child by discussing the child's development and culture. You may need to refer to the child's enrollment file. Spend 30 minutes on each child.

Development
A. Large and small muscle

B. Language

C. Intellectual

D. Emotional

E. Social

Culture

A. Cultural background and customs

B. Child's home life

C. Child's favorite foods

D. Child's preferred way of expressing self and comforting himself/herself

E. Favorite objects, toys, things to talk about - in other words what does this child enjoy?

F. Child's favorite areas in the center, favorite activity

If you were going to plan a day just for this child, what would it be like? What would you do when the child arrived? What would be the sequence and duration of the activities?

Adapted from Leslie R. Williams and Yvonne DeGaetano, *Alerta: A Multicultural, Bilingual Approach to Teaching Young Children*, 1985.

Many different people live in our community.
People work together and help one another.
Some things are real and some are pretend.
Some things are fair and some things are unfair.
People have different points of view.

Developmentally appropriate multicultural activities will also help children acquire these social and cognitive skills:

Social skills:

noticing and labeling feelings	
showing pride in oneself	protecting oneself
being a friend	avoiding name calling
being part of a group	resolving conflicts
decision-making	helping others
working together, cooperation	

Cognitive skills:

observing	naming
describing	classifying
matching	differentiating
comparing	predicting
gathering information	explaining
suggesting alternatives	problem solving

(Kendall 1983, 43-4, and Ramsey 1987)

Introducing Multicultural Activities

As teachers, we spend long hours making learning games, teaching aides, and rotating materials. Sometimes, we become frustrated that children do not notice or use the materials. How we introduce new materials and activities is an important part of teaching. Take time to introduce materials and activities to children. A clear introduction builds interest and helps children be successful. Keep in mind these two ideas when introducing multicultural activities and materials.

1. Help children appreciate multicultural materials by introducing them as such. Talk about who the object belongs to, who made it, where it came from, and how it is used. Children may not remember the information, but will "catch" the feeling that this is something important and special. Sensing the teacher's interest and respect increases children's interest in activities and materials (Texas Department of Human Services 1985).

2. When introducing materials or activities, avoid making sweeping generalizations. For example, don't say: "All Japanese people eat with chopsticks." or "All Black people love to dance." These kinds of statements are stereotypical. Whenever possible, introduce a multicultural activity or material in relation to a person or a family that the children know, such as: "Sato's family is Japanese and sometimes they eat with chopsticks" (Derman-Sparks 1989).

Multicultural Activity Ideas

The following activities illustrate how you can take common early childhood materials and activities and adapt them to multicultural concepts. These activities are designed to help children explore, examine, and talk about their feelings and perceptions. Because some children may respond negatively or in a biased manner, I've included a list at the beginning of each content area of comments children might make while participating in these activities. You might want to think about how you would respond to such comments before offering the activities to the children in your class. (See Chapter 9 for suggestions on how to handle these comments.)

These activities are developmentally appropriate for preschool and kindergarten children. All of the activities may not be appropriate for an individual child or for your particular group of children. Some may be too simple, others too difficult. What works with a group of three year olds may not work with a group of five year olds. Use discretion in selecting which activities to include in your curriculum. Refer to Chapter 7 if you are unsure about the appropriateness of an activity.

Explore the Concept of Skin Color

Be prepared for comments such as: Does my skin have color? Why does her skin have two colors? I want to make his color. I'm gonna make me black. I don't like my color. I white—I don't have a color. Black is for bad guys. Brown is poopy on her. His skin's not brown. Are you black? She's mostly white.

Mixing Playdough

Themes	I'm Me and I'm Special, Alike and Different, Colors, Five Senses, Light and Dark, Bodies, Changes
Goal	To help children explore shades of skin color by making and mixing different colors of playdough.
Materials Needed	Mixing bowls, measuring cups, measuring spoons, large spoon for stirring, flour, salt, alum, oil, powder tempera paint or cake decorators (paste) food coloring.
Description	With the children prepare five batches of playdough, one in each of the following colors: black, brown, red, yellow, white. Use this recipe or one you're familiar with.

Playdough Recipe
2 C. flour
1/2 C. salt
2 T. alum
1-1/2 C. warm water
1 T. oil
paste food coloring or powder tempera paint

Instructions: Mix 1–3 T. of powder tempera with the liquid ingredients. Stir liquids into the dry ingredients. Knead until smooth. Store in an airtight container.

Tell the children there are five different colors of playdough and they can make different colors by mixing two or three colors together. For example, combining red playdough with white playdough will make pink playdough. Ask the children to look at the color of their skin. Encourage them to mix different colors of playdough so that their ball of playdough matches their skin color. As the children experiment with combining the playdough, talk with them about the concepts of new colors, shades of color, and lighter and darker.

Variations

1. Make a recipe chart that shows how to mix colors.

2. Put each child's ball of skin-colored playdough in a plastic bag and allow them to take it home.

3. During group time, see if the children can order the balls of playdough from light to dark.

4. Leave the five colors of playdough out on the art shelf for two weeks so that children can continue to experiment with mixing colors to match their skin color.

Fingerpaint Mix-Up

Themes

I'm Me and I'm Special, Changes, Alike and Different, Five Senses, Light and Dark, Bodies

Goal

To help children explore shades of skin color by combining colors as they fingerpaint.

Materials

Liquid starch, black, brown, red, yellow, and white powder tempera paint, fingerpaint paper, paint smocks, small plastic bowls, teaspoons.

Description

Put a small amount of each color of powder tempera paint into bowls and set them out on a table. Ask the children to put on a paint smock to protect their clothes. Show the children the five colors of paint. Ask them, "What do you think will happen if you mix the colors together?" Then ask the children to look at their skin color. Encourage them to mix the colors so that the fingerpaint matches the color of their skin. Give each child a piece of fingerpaint paper and pour approximately 3 tablespoons of liquid starch directly onto the paper. Tell the children they can spoon the powder tempera onto their paper and mix the colors and starch together with their hands. Compare the color of the fingerpaint with each child's skin color and ask them questions to help them figure out how to make fingerpaint the same color as their skin.

Variations

1. After the painting has dried, encourage the children to draw a face on their artwork.

2. Allow the children to fingerpaint directly on the table. When they are finished, lay a piece of paper on top of the area. Press down and lift the paper off quickly, making a print of the finger painting. This gives children a chance to freely experiment without using up a lot of paper.

Color Collage

Themes	Colors, Light and Dark, Day and Night
Goal	To help children associate positive images and feelings with the color black.
Materials	Gray construction paper, magazines, scissors, glue.
Description	Set out magazines and scissors on a table. Ask the children to think of things they like that are black in color. Talk about how there are many wonderful things in our world that are black. Give each child a piece of gray construction paper. Talk about how the color gray comes from mixing black with white. Encourage the children to go through the magazines and cut out pictures of their favorite black things. Allow the children to glue their pictures to the paper any way they choose.
Variations	1. Repeat the activity focusing on the color brown. Use tan construction paper instead of gray.
	2. Go on a "color walk" to look for all of the beautiful black and brown things in the world
	3. Have a "Black Day" at school where everyone wears black and brings a favorite black object to school.
	4. Set up a discovery table with black objects. Encourage the children to put the objects next to their skin.
	5. Make and use black and brown playdough.

Skin Color Match-Ups

Themes

I'm Me and I'm Special, Alike and Different, Colors, Clothes We Wear, Light and Dark, Bodies

Goal

To help children explore the range of skin color.

Materials

Collection of nylon knee-hi stockings in many shades of tan, black, white, pink, yellow, and red.

Description

Set out the collection of knee hi's at the discovery table or introduce them to the children at group time. Tell the children you have stockings in many different shades of brown and some stockings in other colors. Encourage the children to try them on their hands and arms or their feet and legs. Ask these questions to help the children increase their awareness of skin color: "Can you find a stocking that is the same color as your skin?" "What color is that stocking you have on your arm?" "Try the _____ stocking. Is it lighter or darker than your own skin?"

Variations

1. Set out stockings in the dramatic play area.

2. Have children match the same colored stockings to make a pair.

3. Have the children order the stockings from light to dark.

4. Talk about how no one's skin color is purely white, pink, yellow, or red.

Face Masks

Themes	I'm Me and I'm Special, Friends, Families, Changes, Alike and Different, Colors, Folk Tales, Light and Dark, Bodies
Goal	To help children explore and express their feelings about differences of skin color through creative dramatics.
Materials	Poster board, tempera paint, clear contact paper, scissors, wax crayons, paper towels.
Description	Cut four to six masks out of poster board. Paint each mask a different shade of tan to correspond with the skin colors represented in the classroom. When the masks are dry, cover both sides with clear contact paper. Introduce the masks during group time. Tell the children that they may take the masks, draw faces on them, and use them during free play. Show them how to wipe off the crayon "face" with a paper towel when they are done or want to change the expression. Encourage the children to form small groups to use the masks in their dramatic play.
Variations	1. Use the masks to tell a story or retell a discriminatory incident in the classroom. Change roles by switching masks. 2. Set out full-length mirror so that children can see themselves.

Sock Puppets

Themes	I'm Me and I'm Special, Boys and Girls, Friends, Alike and Different, Colors, Feelings, Folk Tales, Books, Bodies
Goals	To give children an opportunity to make a three dimensional object to represent themselves and to gain skills in verbal self-expression.
Materials	Collection of tan, beige, cream, brown, peach, and other skin-colored socks; felt scraps, assorted fabric trim, yarn, buttons, glue, mirrors.
Description	Say to the children, "I brought some materials so that you can make a sock puppet that looks just like you." Let the children select the color of sock they want to use for making a puppet. Encourage them to choose one that is like their skin color. Set out the mirror and materials on a table. The children may want to look in the mirror when deciding how to make their puppet's facial features and hair. Talk about the similarities and differences between the puppets. For example, you could say, "Each puppet is different because it looks like the person who is making it."
Variation	Set up or make a puppet stage and encourage the children to act out a story or classroom situation.

Light and Dark

Themes	Alike and Different, Colors, Light and Dark, Bodies
Goals	To help children explore the concepts of light and dark; to help children notice the variations of skin color in terms of light and dark.
Materials	Colors Around Us study prints (available through Afro-American Publishing company—see Chapter 4) or your own set of pictures of people with different skin color, easel, easel paper, paint brushes, four shades of the same color paint (preferably brown).
Description	During group time show the children the pictures of people with different skin color. Tell the children to look at their skin. Ask such questions as: "Is your skin light or dark?" "Does it ever get darker than it is now?" "Does it ever get lighter?" Also ask the children if they know how to make a color darker or how to make a color lighter. Show them the four containers of paint. Talk about how each container holds a different shade of the color brown. Ask, "Which one is the lightest?" and "Which one is the darkest?" Tell the children that they can experiment with the light and dark shades of paint at the easel during free choice play.
Variations	1. Use paint swatches instead of a picture set.
	2. Older children can experiment with mixing shades of paint for use at the easel. Have them choose a color and slowly add white paint to create lighter shades. This gives children the experience of beginning with dark and changing it to light.
	(NOTE: A child may express discomfort by saying, "I want a lighter color." Consider this response: "Are you wanting your skin to be lighter? What do you like about light colored skin?" Once you discover what the child is responding to, you can provide accurate information.)

What Color Are You?

Themes   Colors, Bodies, I'm Me and I'm Special, Our Community

Goal   To help children recognize and name skin color.

Materials   Pictures of people from a variety of racial groups (or the "Colors Around Us" study prints).

Description   Hold up one picture at a time. Ask such questions as: "Who can tell me about this picture?" "Who is this person?" "Is this person a boy or a girl?" "How do you know?" "What color is this person's skin?" "What color is their hair?" "Where do you think this person lives?" Write down the children's answers. Make a bulletin board display by posting the pictures along with the children's descriptions.

Variation   Mix up the pictures and lay them face down. Select a child to come up and choose a picture from the pile. Ask the child to show it to the class and describe the person in the picture.

How Do You Feel About Color?

Themes   Colors, Feelings, Books

Goal   To help children express the feelings they associate with different colors.

Materials   Colored construction paper, felt-tip pen, stapler.

Description   Begin by asking all of the children wearing the color blue to stand up. Tell them to look at their blue clothes. Ask, "What do you think of when you see the color blue?" and "How do you feel when you see the color blue?" Repeat this game with many colors. Include skin colors like tan, brown, black, and peach.

Tell the children they can make a color book. Work with the children one at a time. Ask them what they are reminded of when they see each color and how it makes them feel. Write down their words on that colored sheet of construction paper. Put the sheets of paper together and staple the corner to make a simple flip book.

Variation   1. Write down the children's responses and add them to a bulletin board about color.

2. Show the children the "Colors Around Us" study prints. (Available through Afro-American Publishing Co. See classroom Resources in Chapter 4.)

3. Teach the children the names of colors in another language.

Notice Physical Characteristics

Be prepared for comments such as: Can he see with those eyes? She got fuzzy hair. Boy, is he fat. Am I darker than her? Why is he so little? Why is she darker? I'm bigger than you. You got funny eyes. What's wrong with him? White is best. I don't want to touch her. Ugh, her hairs funny. Do black people have freckles?

Draw Me/Draw You	
Themes	I'm Me and I'm Special, Friends, Alike and Different, Five Senses
Goal	To help children notice facial features and the uniqueness of each person.
Materials	Drawing paper, felt-tip pens, crayons.
Description	Have the children find a partner and ask them to sit across from one another at the table. Encourage the children to draw a picture of their partner's face. Ask them to look at their partner. Then ask: "What color is his skin? What color are her eyes? Does he have freckles? What color is her hair? How long is his hair? Is her hair straight or curly?" The drawing probably won't look like the partner. That's all right because it's the looking at the features of another person that is important. Ask the children to exchange the drawings when they are done.
Variations	1. Have the children describe themselves to each other before they begin drawing. 2. Have the children share their drawings with the class at group time. 3. Play a guessing game during group time by having the children look at the drawing and guess who it is.

Body Paintings

Themes	I'm Me and I'm Special, Boys and Girls, Alike and Different, Colors, Bodies
Goal	To help children become aware of their body, skin color, and facial features.
Materials	Unbreakable full-length mirror, tempera paint mixed with soap, paint brushes, paint containers.
Description	This is an activity for children to do one at a time. Have the child stand in front of the mirror. Ask the child to draw his body on the mirror using a paintbrush and paint. Encourage the child to trace the outline of the body first and then fill it in. Talk with the child about his body shape and physical features.
Variations	1. Put a piece of clear plastic film over the mirror. This allows the child to save the picture. Put it up to the sunlight or on a window and see the light come through.
	2. Ask the child to stand up against the mirror and then trace her body. The child then colors it in.
	3. Make a body sculpture. Have the children lay on butcher paper and trace their bodies. Give them paint, crayons, or felt-tip pens to color it in. When the drawing is complete, put a plain sheet of butcher paper underneath. Cut out the body drawing, cutting both sheets of paper at the same time. Staple the two "bodies" together around the edges and stuff with newspaper.

Touching Game

Themes   Boys and Girls, Friends, Alike and Different, Bodies, Five Senses

Goal   To help children notice the physical characteristics of their classmates.

Materials   A large open space for a group game.

Description   Tell the children that they are going to play a group game about finding and touching body parts. Have everyone stand up. Ask the children to touch their hands to their heads. Say, "Now I will ask you to use your hand to touch a friend. When I say, Touch an arm, find a friend and touch their arm with your hand." Continue the game by saying, "Touch someone's _____," or "Touch someone with _____." Start with a few familiar body parts. Then focus on physical characteristics related to skin color and race such as brown skin, black hair, blonde hair, freckles, round eyes, or dark skin, light skin, curly hair, straight hair. Use characteristics of the children in the class. Depending on the cultures of the children in your classroom, you might want to avoid suggesting children touch each other on the head.

Variation   Choose some physical characteristics that are not represented in your classroom and notice how the children respond.

Thumbprints

Themes   I'm Me and I'm Special, Alike and Different, Five Senses, Bodies, Our Community

Goals   To help children discover that all people have physical characteristics that make them unique and different from everyone else.

Materials   White paper (3 x 5 cards), black ink pad, pen, magnifying glass.

Procedure   Encourage the children to make prints of their thumbs by pressing their thumb on the ink pad and then on the paper. Label each print with the child's name. At group time, show the children the prints. Talk about how everyone has patterns of lines on the skin of their fingers, how each person has a different pattern, and how each person's fingerprints are different from everyone else's. No two are alike. Set out the prints and a magnifying glass on the table so the children can examine the similarities and differences in the fingerprints.

Variation   Make two sets of prints for each child. Mix them up and see if the children can match them.

Hair

Themes   I'm Me and I'm Special, Boys and Girls, Alike and Different, Clothes We Wear, Bodies

Goal   To help children notice hair as a distinguishing physical characteristic and discover that some people express their culture through hair style.

Materials   Pictures of a variety of people with different hairstyles, a hand mirror, empty hair care containers, wigs, scarves, turbans, rubber bands, hair clips, combs, old hair dryers, old curling irons, old crimping irons.

Description   Show pictures of different hairstyles to the children. Ask them to touch their hair. Talk about how hair has texture and curl; how some people have fine hair and some people have coarse hair. Some people have straight hair and other people have curly hair. Pass around the mirror so that children can look at their hair. Talk about how people differ in the color and length of their hair. Set out hair care materials in the dramatic play area for children to use during free choice play.

Variation   As an introduction to the activity, read the book *Cornrows* by C. Yarbrough (New York: Putnam, 1979).

Photo Masks

Themes	I'm Me and I'm Special, Boys and Girls, Friends, Changes, Alike and Different, Feelings
Goal	To help children explore diversity by taking on another person's identity through role playing.
Materials	Close-up photographs of people's faces (choose people in your center that exemplify a variety of differences), rubber cement, poster board, hole punch, scissors, string.
Description	Have the photos enlarged to 8" x 10". Cut out the photo around the hair and face. Mount the photo on poster board using rubber cement. Punch a hole on both sides above the ear. Tie a 12-inch piece of string through each hole. Introduce the masks at group time. Set them out on a "discovery table" with a mirror, or in the dramatic play area. Observe the children and notice their conversations as they try on different masks.
Variation	Record the children's voices or write down what they say as they take on other people's identities. (Adapted from *Constructive Play*, 1984. Forman and Hill.)

Discovering My Body

Themes   Bodies, I'm Me and I'm Special, Changes, Alike and Different

Goal   To help children learn about their bodies and compare their
                      height, weight, skin color, hair, and facial features with those of
                      their classmates.

Materials   Mirrors, magnifying glasses, scale, tape measure.

Description   Set mirrors, magnifying glasses, scale, and tape measure out on a
                      table for children to explore. Encourage them to use the materials
                      to find out about their bodies. Children can use the tape measure
                      to measure each other's bodies. Talk about similarities and
                      differences between children.

Variations   1. Make a height and weight chart of all the children in the class.
                      Take measurements throughout the year to help children become
                      aware of changes in their bodies.

                      2. Write down children's words as they describe themselves and
                      their bodies.

                      3. Make a poster for each child that includes his or her height,
                      weight, and a self-description.

Face Puzzles

Themes	I'm Me and I'm Special, Bodies, Alike and Different, Friends
Goal	To help children discover that each person's face is unique because of the color and shape of its features, but that all faces are similar because the features are in the same place on each person.
Materials	Camera, film, rubber cement, poster board or foam core, mat knife or Exacto knife, pencil, ruler.
Description	Take a close-up photo of each child's face. Have the photos enlarged to 8" x 10". Glue the photo to the foam core and let dry. Using a ruler, mark off the photo in fourths vertically and horizontally. With a pencil, lightly draw lines for cutting out the pieces. This results in sixteen 2-inch squares. Cut out the pieces with the Exacto knife and put the child's name or initials on the back of each piece. During group time, give the pieces to each child in a plastic bag. Encourage them to try to put together their face puzzle. As they work on their own puzzle, talk about where the eyes, nose, and mouth are located on a person's face. When children have completed their puzzle, ask them to hold up the piece that shows their mouth. Talk about how each person's mouth is different. Continue with the other facial features.
Variations	1. Combine three or four puzzles and see if children can unscramble them and make the correct faces. 2. Set the puzzle pieces out in a tub and let children freely explore putting the pieces together to create different faces.

Line Up

Themes

Bodies, I'm Me and I'm Special, Friends, Alike and Different

Goal

To help children recognize their own body shape, notice other people's body shapes, and represent their physical characteristics.

Materials

Large sheet of butcher paper, masking tape, felt-tip marker, crayons.

Description

Tape up the butcher paper on a wall or fence. Have the entire class line up next to one another with their backs to the paper. Draw around their bodies with a felt-tip pen. The children can stand away from the wall as soon as you finish tracing their body. They'll enjoy looking at their outline as well as watching you trace the rest of the class. When finished, encourage the children to look at the mural. Can they recognize each person's outline? How do they know? Distribute crayons or markers and encourage the children to draw their face, color in their skin and hair, and color in their clothes. Display the mural in the hallway or classroom.

Variation

As a group decide how each person's body should be colored in.

Felt Friends

Themes	I'm Me and I'm Special, Bodies, Boys and Girls, Alike and Different, Families, Colors, Feelings, Clothes We Wear
Goal	To help children explore ideas about how they look.
Materials	Felt squares in a variety of skin colors, gingerbread cookie cutter, scissors, fine tip black felt-tip marker, assorted felt scraps, flannel board.
Description	Show children the different colors of felt and tell them that you are going to make a felt doll for each of them to use on the flannel board. Say, "Pick which color of felt is most like the color of your skin."
	Use the cookie cutter to trace the doll on the felt and cut it out. Write the child's name on the back of the doll. Make clothes for the dolls out of the felt scraps. Introduce the dolls to the class during a group time. See if the children can match the doll with the child. Set the dolls and the flannel board out during free play.
Variations	1. Make a small flannel board for each child.
	2. Cut out, mount, and laminate magazine illustrations to make scenery and props to use with felt friends.
	3. Make a felt doll to represent each family member.

People Paper Dolls

Themes   I'm Me and I'm Special, Boys and Girls, Friends, Bodies, Alike and Different, Feelings

Goal   To help children increase their self-awareness and explore their relationships with people who are different.

Materials   Camera, film, cardboard, 1-inch diameter half-round moulding, Exacto knife, saw, rubber cement.

Description   Take a full-length picture of each child. Have it enlarged so that it measures 10 inches high. Mount the photo on cardboard and cut it out with an Exacto knife. Cut a short piece (2 inches) of moulding and saw a groove in the rounded side for a stand. Slide the paper doll into the groove. Set the dolls out in the block area or with the doll house. Encourage children to create situations and dramas with their dolls.

Variations   1. Use the dolls to act out conflicts between children.

2. Make dolls of people from different cultures.

3. Make a doll for each member of a family.

I'm Special Book

Themes	I'm Me and I'm Special, Friends, Books, Alike and Different
Goal	To help children feel good about themselves and notice how each of the children in the class is special.
Materials	Construction paper (12" x 18"), yarn, hole punch, camera, film, felt-tip marker, glue.
Description	Make a book for each child by folding three sheets of construction paper in half. Punch holes 1/2-inch from the fold. Thread the yarn through the hole and tie in a bow to secure the book. Take a photograph of each child and glue it to the cover. Fill the book with information about and photographs of the child. Include physical characteristics (height, weight, skin color, eye color), favorite toys, family size and members, languages spoken at home, pets, nickname, birth date, and age. Set the "I'm Special" books in the classroom's book corner for all the children to look at and read.
Variations	1. Make the book so that it can be filled in at home by the parent and child. 2. Make a book of the entire class with a page or two for each child.

Explore Racial and Ethnic Constancy

Be prepared for comments such as: When I grow up I'm gonna be white. When I grow up my eyes are gonna be like hers. When I a daddy I won't be brown anymore. Does her color wash off? He just needs to take a bath. She's been in the sun too long.

Family Photos

Themes	Families, Changes, Alike and Different, Clothes We Wear, Bodies
Goal	To help children discover that physical characteristics stay the same throughout life (racial/ethnic constancy).
Materials	Photographs of children's parents, photographs of each child, resealable plastic bags.
Description	Collect photos from the parents, assuring them that they will be returned in a week or two. This activity may bring up questions about different types of families (single parent, gay/lesbian, and blended families). Put them in individual resealable plastic bags for safe keeping. Tell the children they are going to play a guessing game and that you are going to set out the photos of parents for all the children to see. But everyone must be quiet and not tell the others which photo is of their parent. Give each child the photo of himself/herself to hold. One by one ask the children to come up in front of the group with their pictures. Encourage the child to show the photo to the class. Then ask the class to look at the photos of parents. Ask, "Who can guess which photo is of _____'s parents?" Encourage the children to notice hair color, skin color, and other physical similarities. When a correct match has been made, place the child's photo next to the one of the parents. After everyone has had a turn, encourage the children to look at all the pictures. Ask the children, "What do you think you will look like when you grow up?" Talk about how children get their skin color and physical looks from their biological parents. Also talk about how many of our physical characteristics such as skin color and eye color stay the same as we grow older.

Variations

1. You may need to vary this activity if you have adopted or multiracial children in your group. Ask parents how they explain the origin of skin color and physical features to their children.

2. Set out the photos for the children to look at and match on their own.

3. Make a bulletin board display of the photographs at the children's eye level.

4. Make a class book of children's families.

5. Repeat the activity with baby pictures and current photographs of each child.

Washing

Themes	Changes, Colors, Bodies, Five Senses, Light and Dark
Goal	To help children discover that skin color is a physical characteristic that does not wash off.
Materials	Brown finger paint or mud, sink or water table with soapy water, towels.
Description	Encourage the children to fingerpaint. Talk about the brown paint on the children's hands. Notice how it looks on different colors of skin. Ask "What will happen to your skin when you wash your hands?" "Will you wash off your skin color?" "Does it make a difference if your skin is light or dark?" Talk about how skin color doesn't wash off and how it always stays the same.
Variations	1. Read the book *The Marvelous Mud Washing Machine* by Patty Wolcott (New York: Scholastic Books, 1974). 2. Experiment with washing dolls, rocks, and other objects. 3. Make a list of things that keep their color when washed and things that lose their color when washed.

Adapted from Derman-Sparks: *Anti-Bias Curriculum.* 1989.

Activities to Help Children Explore Similarities and Differences

Be prepared for such comments as: His mom and dad aren't the same. She's different from me. He can't be your dad. That can't be your mom. Look at him —he's really different. What's wrong with her? Why does he look that way? Why does she talk funny? He doesn't smell right.

Same As Me	
Themes	Alike and Different, Our Community, Bodies, Friends
Goal	To help children identify ways in which people are similar.
Materials	One large piece of paper, felt-tip marker.
Description	Display the paper on a wall. Ask the children to look around at all of the people in the classroom. Say, "Look at their faces and look at their bodies. Let's see if we can name all of the ways we are like one another." Ask the group, "What is one way that our bodies are the same?" Ask an individual child, "Kimong, what is one way that your body is the same as Asumpta's body?" Write the children's answers on the paper. When the list is complete, show the children pictures of people from other cultures. Ask the children, "How is this person like you?"
Variation	Repeat the activity focusing on differences.

Which One Is Different?

Themes   Alike and Different, Boys and Girls, Bodies, Colors, Places
People Live, Toys and Games, Clothes We Wear, Food We Eat

Goal   To help children recognize differences in people and objects.

Materials   Strips of oak tag or poster board (4" x 20"), magazine pictures,
rubber cement, clear contact paper.

Description   For each strip, draw or glue on four pictures that are similar,
discarding the one that is different. Here are some examples:

1. four pictures of African American children
2. four pictures of an Hispanic American child
3. four pictures of different Asian American children
4. four pictures of an Euro-American child

Start with pictures that show obvious differences. Later, add
pictures with less distinct differences. Encourage the children to
see if they can find both similarities and differences among the
pictures. Ask the child to find the ways in which the people in
the picture are alike.

Variations   1. Older children can make their own "alike" and "different"
picture strips.

2. Trace appropriate drawings or pictures of people. Duplicate
them on a copying machine and color them in.

3. Also use picture strips of objects like Native American baskets
or pottery.

Sound Choice

Themes	I'm Me and I'm Special, Boys and Girls, Friends, Five Senses, Alike and Different
Goal	To help children identify people by the sound of their voices and to notice differences in how people speak.
Materials	Cassette tape recorder, blank cassette tape.
Description	Tape the children's voices one at a time. With a small group of children play the tape and see if they can guess whose voice they hear on the cassette tape. Ask them how they know who it was.
Variations	1. Blindfold children and see if they can identify their friends by the sound of their voices. 2. Tape parents and staff in addition to children. 3. Make a tape of people speaking in different languages and accents. Include someone speaking languages of the cultures represented in your program or community.

Match-Ups

Themes	Families, Our Community, Alike and Different, Places People Live, Toys and Games, Transportation, Clothes We Wear, Food We Eat, Holidays and Celebrations
Goal	To help children match people of different cultures with objects from their culture.
Materials	Photographs of people from various cultures, real objects from each culture or a photograph of common objects, rubber cement, oak tag or poster board, fine felt-tip marker.
Description	Make five sets of matching cards by cutting out ten 4" x 6" oak tag rectangles. Draw or glue a photograph of a person onto one of the cards and an object from that person's culture on the other card. Use current examples and avoid pictures of people in their native costumes. Show the children the pictures of the objects. Talk about how these are things that people use. Show the children the pictures of the people. Talk about where these people come from and how they live. Set the cards face up in two sets: objects and people. Tell the children that one of the objects matches one of the people. Encourage the children to match a person with an object. Choose people and objects that the children are already familiar with. Note, however, that you should not use this activity to introduce a culture.

Patterns

Themes   Alike and Different, Colors, Folk Tales, Books, Clothes We Wear

Goal   To help children recognize cultural design patterns.

Materials   Oak tag or poster board, scissors, tracing paper, pencil, markers or crayons, clear contact paper.

Description Every culture uses colorful design patterns. These patterns may be found on fabric used for native dress, beadwork, tapestry, pottery, or others forms of artwork. Find and copy simple design patterns onto 4" x 6" pieces of oak tag. Make two cards of each pattern. Color the designs using colors that would normally appear on that type of art. Write the name of the pattern and the culture that it comes from on the back of the card. Cover the cards with contact paper. Tell the children you have a new matching game for them. Encourage them to match the pattern cards. Talk about the different designs and the cultures that they come from.

Variations 1. Play the game Concentration with the cards.

2. Make a number of sets and play the game Go Fish with the cards.

Daily Life and Celebrations

Themes
Alike and Different, Folk Tales, Dance and Movement, Clothes We Wear, Holiday and Celebrations

Goal
To help children learn to tell the difference between the daily dress and ethnic dress of people.

Materials
Manila file folder, 4" x 6" or 5" x 8" index cards, 5" x 8" manila clasp envelope, felt-tip markers, clear contact paper, magazine pictures, rubber cement.

Description
Make a file folder game for children to sort pictures of people into two categories: everyday life and celebrations. Open up the file folder. Label the left side "Everyday Life" and glue on magazine pictures that represent everyday life. Label the right side "Celebrations" and glue on magazine pictures that show people celebrating special occasions. Collect 20 pictures of people of different cultures in daily life activities (wearing street clothes, living in the here and now) and celebrating special events (wearing ethnic costumes). Glue each picture to an index card. Write the culture and the event on the back of the card. Cover both the file folder and the index cards with clear contact paper. Attach the small manila envelope to the outside of the file folder with a metal fastener. Store the cards in the envelope. Introduce the game to the children during a group time and set it out for the children to use during free play.

Variations
Play the game as a group with each child taking a turn and the others watching.

Mothers and Babies

Themes   Families, Alike and Different, Changes, Bodies, Animals, Pets

Goal   To help children discover that parents and children are members of the same race and share the same cultural heritage, even though they may look different.

Materials   Photographs of mothers and babies from various cultures, a photograph of a mother cat with kittens, rubber cement, oak tag or poster board, clear contact paper.

Description   Cut 23 4" x 6" rectangles out of oak tag or poster board. Cut out a magazine picture of a mother (woman that looks like a mother) from each of the following racial groups: Hispanic, Black, Native American, Asian, and Euro-American. Glue each picture to an index card. Find four pictures of babies from each of the racial groups and mount them on the oak tag cards. Tell the children you have a new matching game for them. Set out the five pictures of mothers. Ask the children, "How are these mothers different from each other?" Show the children the cards with the pictures of babies. Encourage the children to match the picture of the baby with the mother. Ask them, "How do you know that baby belongs to that mother?" Show the children a picture of a mother cat with kittens. Talk about how even though the kittens look different from the mother cat, they are still her kittens.

Variations   1. Cut out or draw pictures of objects used by different cultures to care for babies such as baby carriers and toys. Add these cards to the game.

2. Introduce children to lullabies from various cultures.

Real and Pretend

Themes

Feelings, Holidays and Celebrations

Goal

To help children tell the difference between real people and discriminatory pretend images of people.

Materials

Manila file folder, 4" x 6" or 5" x 8" index cards, 5" x 8" manila clasp envelope, felt-tip markers, clear contact paper, magazine pictures, greeting cards, rubber cement, metal fastener.

Description

Make a manila file folder game. Label one side of the folder "Real" and the other side "Pretend." Underneath each word, glue pictures to illustrate the concept. Make a number of cards (16 or more) with actual pictures of people from various cultures. On an equal number of the cards, glue cartoons and other pretend images of people. Example: animals wearing a feather head dress or a sombrero. Introduce the game by asking such questions as: "How do you know if something is real?" "How do you know if a person is real?" "How do you know if something is pretend?" Talk about pretend pictures of people, and how it can be hard to tell if the person in the picture is real. Some pictures make animals look like people. Encourage the children to look at the picture cards and see if they can sort them. (Adapted from Derman-Sparks: *Anti-Bias Curriculum*, 1989.)

Variation

Tell the children that when animals are dressed up to look like people they are really making fun of people. Say, "These pretend pictures hurt people's feelings and make people mad because they are not true."

Guess Who?

Themes   Bodies, Five Senses, Friends, Alike and Different

Goal   To help children explore similarities and differences of facial features.

Material   Scarf or mask for a blindfold.

Description   Introduce this activity by talking with the children about the ways in which people are different from one another. For example, our hair is different. The shape and size of people's eyes, nose, and mouth are different. When we use our eyes, we see that people look different from one another. We can also know that people are different by feeling their face and body with our hands. Tell the children they can play a guessing game. One person is blindfolded and tries to guess who children are by touching and feeling. Ask, "How did you know?" when a child guesses the identity of a classmate.

Variation   Have children feel their own faces and bodies before the game begins.

We're All Human

Themes   Boys and Girls, Friends, Families, Alike and Different, Places People Live

Goal   To help children explore the similarities among all people regardless of race or culture.

Materials   Pictures of children from around the world in everyday settings, books about children from other cultures.

Description   Display the pictures on a bulletin board near the book corner or group area. Show the children the pictures and talk about them. Read two stories about children from other cultures. Say, "People live in many different places. People have different colored skin and different colors of eyes. But in many important ways, we are all alike." Ask the children if they can think of some ways that they are like the children in the story. Children's answers may include: "We have mommies and daddies, go to sleep, play, go to school, eat, wear clothes, have families, go to work, cry, get sad." End the group discussion by talking about how people are alike even though they look different and live in different places.

Group Tree

Themes   I'm Me and I'm Special, Friends, Our Community, Alike and Different

Goal   To help children become aware of racial groups and become aware that groups are made of individual people.

Materials   Five dead tree branches, five large coffee cans, sand or plaster of paris, magazines, scissors, glue, construction paper, hole punch, yarn, photographs of each child and staff members.

Description   Make five "trees" by securing each branch in a can filled with sand or plaster of paris. Let the plaster of paris dry and harden. Bring the "trees" to group time. Introduce them by explaining the concept of a group: groups are more than two people, a family is a group, and our class is a group. Each of the "trees" is like a group: there is a "tree" for Blacks, Hispanics, Asians, Native Americans, and Euro-Americans. One by one show the class a photo of each child and staff member. As a group, decide which tree to hang the photo on. If the class is not multicultural and some of the trees are bare, talk about how no children from these ethnic groups are in your class, but these people do live in your city and go to another school. Tell the children there will be magazines, scissors, glue, and construction paper out in the art area during free choice time. The children can cut out pictures of people and hang them on the appropriate "tree." Leave the "trees" out for a few weeks so that children can keep adding pictures to them.

Variation   Make group posters instead of "trees."

Develop Social Skills

Be prepared for such comments as: But that's what my dad calls them. I'm not your friend—you yucky. Ooooh yuck! I'm not gonna try that. They do too look like that. Really, they will hurt you. Nope, he can't be my friend. There's nobody here that looks like me.

Victim Aid	
Themes	Friends, Feelings
Goal	To help children realize that name calling and discriminating against people based on their physical characteristics is hurtful.
Materials	Band-Aid strips
Description	Intervene every time a child is discriminated against either by name calling or because of physical characteristics. Bring the children together. Ask the victim, "How does it feel to be called _____?" Talk about how name calling makes us sad, and it hurts our feelings. Ask the victim what she would like to say to the child making discriminatory remarks, ask the child how you can help. Give the child a Band-Aid strips for their "owie" and tell the child they can put it anywhere on their body they want.

How Would You Feel If...?

Themes   Friends, Feelings

Goal   To help children become aware of feelings associated with racism and increase their sensitivity to the feelings of others.

Materials   Oak tag, scissors, metal fastener, fine-tip marker, multicultural photographs or pictures of people in various everyday settings.

Description   Cut an 8-inch circle out of oak tag. Divide the circle into six sections. In each section draw one face to represent the following emotions: happy, sad, afraid, angry, ashamed, proud. Label the drawings. Make a spinner by cutting an arrow out of the oak tag and attach it to the center of the circle with the metal fastener. Show the child one of the teaching pictures and tell them a simple story about what is happening in the picture. Example: Two boys, Jake and Ta-coumba, are painting at the easel. Jake looks around to see what Ta-coumba is painting. He says, "You're not my friend. You yucky. You muddy." Ask the children, "How do you think Ta-coumba felt when Jake said he was muddy because he is Black? How would you feel if someone called you muddy?" Pass the spinner around so that each child can make the spinner point to the picture and show the other children how they would feel in this situation.

Variation   Discuss actual situations from your classroom using the spinner.

What Would You Do If...?

Themes   Friends, Feelings, Heroes

Goal   To help children explore how they might respond to people who are different or respond when treated unfairly.

Materials   Teaching pictures that show a variety of people in everyday situations.

Description   Show the children one of the pictures. Describe the situation. For example: It's snack time and Tara doesn't want to sit next to Loann because her eyes are funny. Ask the children, "What would you do if you were Loann? How do you think she feels? Is it fair to not like someone because of their eyes?"

Variation   Use the photo paper dolls to tell a story for children to think about.

Try It, You'll Like It

Themes   I'm Me and I'm Special, Changes, Alike and Different

Goal   To help children accept new and different experiences.

Materials   Selection of foods that may be unfamiliar to children (kiwi, mango, papaya, pomegranate, jicama, date), knife, napkins.

Description   Introduce the activity by telling the children you brought some foods that may be new to them. Ask them if they can think of ways to get to know these foods? Answers might include, "We could touch them, smell them, taste them, hold them, look inside them." Focus the conversation on being open and trying new things. Ask the children what would happen if you said "Yucky" and walked away? Explain how we miss out on a lot when we are afraid or don't like new things. Encourage the children to explore the foods with their senses. Cut the fruit open and let the children taste the different foods. Talk about other things that may be new or different in their lives.

Fair and Unfair

Themes	Friends, Feelings, Heroes, Books
Goal	To help children recognize the difference between real and stereotypical objects.
Materials	"Feeling box" or paper sack, collection of real ethnic objects, pictures that accurately portray people from other cultures, stereotypical objects such as greeting cards, cartoons, holiday decorations, and small toy figures.
Description	Mount the pictures on oak tag. Place the pictures and objects in the "feeling box" or a paper sack. Tell the children they can play a guessing game about the many things inside of the "feeling box." Say some of the things are pretend pictures of people. These unfair pictures make people look stupid and silly. They make people sad and seeing them hurts their feelings. These pictures are unfair because what they show is not true. Other pictures and objects in the box are fair because they show people as they really are. Seeing fair pictures make people happy and proud. Encourage children to close their eyes as they put their hand inside the box. Continue to talk about the concepts of unfair and fair as children pull an item from the box. (Adapted from Derman-Sparks, *Anti-Bias Curriculum*, 1989.)
Variations	1. Put all of the pictures and objects into two piles: fair and unfair. 2. Introduce the word stereotype.

True or False

Themes	Alike and Different, Feelings, Books
Goal	To help children tell the difference between true and false images of people.

Materials	Collections of accurate and stereotypical pictures of people. Examples:
	  Asian—coolie hat, person bowing, martial arts, geisha girl.
	  Black—tribal warrior, mammy, athlete
	  Hispanic—sombrero, bandito, siesta, migrant worker
	  Native American—warrior, chief, squaw, papoose

Description	Show the children one picture at a time. Ask, "What is this a picture of? Is this picture true or false?" If a child answers incorrectly, repeat the answer along with a correcting statement. For example, "False. Not all Native Americans are chiefs. And they only wear headdresses with feathers at special ceremonies."
Variations	1. Sort the pictures into two piles: true and false. 2. Encourage the children to look for false pictures in magazines and books.

Superheroes

Themes   Heroes, Friends, Changes, Boys and Girls

Goal   To introduce children to real people who have worked to help people by making wrong things right.

Materials   Visual aids such as picture books, films, pictures of popular cartoon superheroes, pictures of people who have made an important contribution such as: Daniel Inouye, Chief Joseph, Mohandas Gandhi, Tecumseh, Eleanor Roosevelt, Martin Luther King Jr., Jackie Robinson, Nat Turner, Sojourner Truth, Crazy Horse, Cesar Chavez, Phyllis Wheatley, Harriet Tubman, Lucretia Coffin Mott, Susan B. Anthony, Osceola, Booker T. Washington, Paul Robeson, Pontiac, Helen Keller.

Description Show the children pictures of popular cartoon superheroes. Talk with them about how these superheroes appear on TV. Ask the children what they like about the superheroes? Describe heroes as people who make wrong things right. Tell the children that there are real people who are heroes. Say, "Some of the heroes lived a long time ago, but we still remember the good and helpful things they did. Other heroes live today. Sometimes we see them on the news as they work to make the wrong things right. Real heroes care a lot about other people. Real heroes have dreams and hopes of doing important things or making our world a better place. Real heroes work very hard for a long time, and they don't give up." Show the children the teaching pictures and talk about the contributions that each of the real heroes has made. Display the pictures at the children's eye level. Set out books about these people in the book corner.

Variations 1. Celebrate or commemorate the birthdays of real heroes.

2. Ask parents who they would like their children to learn about.

Pick a Friend

Themes   Friends, Alike and Different, Boys and Girls, Feelings

Goal   To help children explore their preferences in picking friends.

Materials   Pictures of boys and girls from a variety of cultures.

Description   Show the children the pictures. As the children are looking at the pictures ask, "Of all these children, who would you like to be your friend?" After the child chooses, follow up with another question like: "What makes this child look like a friend to you?" "Do you see any other children who could be your friend?" "Do you see someone that you would not like to have as a friend?" Notice if the children are selecting potential friends of the same gender and race. Affirm children who willingly choose pictures of children from other cultures as friends.

Variation   Have the child sort the pictures into two groups: friend and not friends. (This activity can be used as a diagnostic tool to help you learn more about children's understanding of differences.)

Just Like Me

Themes   Alike and Different, I'm Me and I'm Special, Friends, Bodies

Goal   To help children explore the concept of alike and different.

Materials   A mirror and variety of pictures of people that represent different cultures, gender, hair color, eye color.

Description   Display the pictures on a wall or table. Ask the children one at a time to pick out all of the pictures of people who look like them. If a child seems unsure, encourage him to look in the mirror. Describe the child's physical characteristics. Then ask, "Do you see any pictures of people with skin color and hair like yours?" Pick out all of the pictures and show them to the child. Talk about the common features between the people in the pictures and the child.

Variations   1. Have the children pick out pictures of people who are not like them.

2. Ask the children to find a partner. Encourage the children to look at their partner and find pictures of people who look like their partner.

Who Is Missing?

Themes   Our Community, Alike and Different, Friends, Five Senses

Goal   To help children recall members of a group.

Materials   A picture of a boy and girl from each of the following groups: African American, Hispanic, Asian, Native American, and Euro-American; or a set of multicultural dolls.

Description   Set all of the pictures face up for the children to see. Pick up the pictures, shuffle them, take one out, and lay the rest back down for the children to see. Ask the children to look at the pictures and guess which one is missing. The child who guesses correctly may shuffle the pictures, pull one out, and lay out the pictures again.

Variations   1. Do the same activity with dolls.

2. Play a memory-matching game by setting out the pictures face down. Have each child take a turn by turning over two cards for all to see. If there is no match (a boy and girl from the same culture), then the cards are put back in their places face down. A child who makes a match may keep the pictures.

Experience Culture in the Context of Daily Life

Be prepared for such comments as: I'm glad I'm not Mexican. I'm glad I don't have to eat that. That's a silly thing. We don't do that at my house. We don't have one of them at my house. This is too my family. That's silly to have lots of moms.

Classroom Scrapbook

Themes
Friends, Books, Holidays and Celebrations, Our Community

Goal
To provide a visual and written record of the year's classroom events and to help children learn about remembering past events through pictures and words.

Materials
Large three-ring binder or bound scrapbook, camera and film.

Description
Use the scrapbook like a diary to capture the celebrations, special events, field trips, visitors, and multicultural activities that go on through the year. The scrapbook must include and represent everyone in the class. Keep a camera handy at all times to take pictures. Children can contribute by dictating their own experiences of classroom activities and drawing pictures.

Variations
1. Allow children and families to check out the book and take it home.

2. Leave it out on the book shelf and encourage children to "read" the stories and retell the events to others.

Family Tree

Themes	I'm Me and I'm Special, Families, Alike and Different
Goal	To help children understand that every family is different.
Materials	A photograph of each child's family, a large piece of butcher paper, a felt-tip marker.
Description	Display the family photos on a bulletin board in the classroom. Together with the children, count the number of people in each child's family. Make a chart showing how many people are in each family. Who has the most people in their family? Who has the smallest number of people in their family? Look at the photographs again. Ask the children to name the family members (mother, father, sister, aunt, grandmother). Write down all of the names a child uses to describe family members. Talk about how there are many different ways of being a family. Some families are small and some are large. Families differ in who lives together and the names they call their members. Include culture when appropriate. For example, Anna's family is German and she calls her aunts "Tanta."

Houses

Themes	Places People Live, Families, Alike and Different, Our Community
Goal	To help children understand that families live in different kinds of dwellings.
Materials	Pictures of different types of houses: homes, apartment buildings, high-rises, houseboats, huts, trailers, tents, cabins, cottages.
Description	Show the children the pictures of different types of houses in which families live. Ask each child to talk about what kind of house their family lives in. Display the pictures in the block area and encourage the children to build different types of houses during free choice time.
Variations	1. Set out boxes and a variety of art materials so that the children can make houses. 2. Take a picture of each child's house or ask the parents to bring in a picture of their child's house. 3. As a class, make a house collage by cutting and pasting pictures of dwellings onto a large sheet of butcher paper.

Smelling Jars

Themes	Five Senses, Alike and Different
Goal	To help children develop their awareness through smell and to introduce children to smells of other cultures.
Materials	Small containers such as margarine tubs, baby food jars, or film containers, a variety of spices, incense, or essential oils (examples include ginger, coriander, anise, five-spice powder, garlic, sesame oil, cilantro, cumin, hot pepper sauce, cardamom, sandalwood, patchouli).
Description	Place one ingredient in each container. Tell the children you have some things for them to smell. Say, "Some of these smells will be familiar. You may have smelled them before at your house. Some of the smells will be new to you." Ask the children to close their eyes and smell the contents of each container. Encourage the children to guess the smell. Talk about how people all over the world use different spices to cook with and have different smells in their homes. Ask the children which ones they like the best.
Variations	1. Make two sets of smelling containers and see if the children can match them. 2. Do a cooking project with some of the spices used in this activity. 3. Make picture labels to go with the smelling jars.

My Family Comes From . . .

Themes   Families, Changes, Places People Live, Books

Goal   To help children understand that every family comes from
                    another place and that every family has a cultural heritage.

Materials   Colored construction paper (12" x 18"), hole punch, yarn, felt-tip
                    pen, photographs of children's families.

Description   Make a book for each child to record his family history and
                    culture. Include photographs of grandparents and extended
                    family members. The book could also include information such
                    as which family members came to the United States, what coun-
                    try they came from, languages spoken at home, simple words in
                    their family's native language, favorite ethnic foods, ethnic
                    customs practiced at home.

Variation   Collect information about families by asking parents to fill out a
                    family questionnaire. (See Chapter 8.)

Multicultural Feast

Themes

Food People Eat, Holidays and Celebrations, Friends, Alike and Different, Families

Goal

To expose children to other types of food and to give them an opportunity to share their culture with others.

Materials

Tables, chairs, eating utensils, plates, and napkins.

Description

Send a note home with the children announcing a special multicultural feast. Ask that each child bring a dish from their family's native culture to share with the rest of the class. This activity works well at Thanksgiving, Christmas, or at the end of the year when children and families have experienced their culture through many other activities.

Variations

1. Invite parents to join the children at the feast.

2. Ask parents for the recipe of their ethnic dish. Make a cookbook and distribute it to all the families.

3. Adapt the recipes so that they can be included in the center's daily food service program.

Slide Show

Themes

Places People Live, Transportation, Clothes We Wear, Friends, Families

Goal

To help children develop an awareness of, and empathy for, people from other parts of the world.

Materials

Slide projector, screen, slides of children, families, family dwellings, and towns from different parts of the world.

Description

Early childhood programs often show films or videos one day a week or when the weather prevents children from going outside. Use this time to expose children to children and families that live far away. Put together your own multicultural slide show using slides from trips and vacations. Select and duplicate slides of people, children, and families involved in everyday activities such as bathing, eating, cooking, playing, sleeping, and working. Don't choose slides that focus on places of interest or famous buildings. If you have not traveled, ask to make copies of slides from friends who have traveled out of the country. If you know someone who is going on a trip, you might buy them a roll of slide film and ask them to take pictures for you.

Variations

1. Make a slide show of people who live in the city or people who live in the country.

2. Make up stories about the lives of the children and families.

3. Go to local ethnic communities that the children may not have an opportunity to learn about (local migrant camp, local reservation, nearest metropolitan area).

4. Visit a multicultural day care center as a source of photographs.

Breads

Themes	Food We Eat, Alike and Different, Five Senses, Holidays and Celebrations
Goals	To help children experience different types of bread.
Materials	Samples of various types of bread (cornbread, tortillas, Mexican sweet bread, matzo, rusk, lefse, pita bread, steamed buns, chapatis, scones, black bread, fry bread, piki bread).
Description	Plan a bread-tasting party for snack time. Talk with the children about how some people from other cultures eat different kinds of bread. Introduce the different breads. Ask the children if they have ever eaten any of them before. Give each child a sample to try. Talk about the name of the bread and where it comes from. Follow up the activity with stories about bread or baking bread for another snack.
Variations	1. Find out what kinds of bread the families from your class eat and use them for exploring different types of breads. 2. Visit an ethnic bakery. 3. Set out jars with different grains and flours and talk about the fact that people eat bread that they make from the grains that they grow. People living in different places grow different grains and make different kinds of bread.

What Do You See?

Themes

Places People Live, Transportation, Books, Friends, Alike and Different, Families, Feelings

Goal

To help children use expressive language and explore their perceptions of people from other cultures.

Materials

A large picture book, pictures of contemporary people from other cultures engaged in everyday activities, large sheets of paper, felt-tip pen.

Description

Read the story to children, emphasizing how the pictures show us what is happening in the story. Hold up one of the pictures for the children to see. Ask the children, "What do you think is happening in this picture?" Encourage the children to tell a story about the people in the picture. Write their stories down on the paper. Display the picture and written stories in the book area.

Variations

1. Stack the pictures face down and invite a child to pick a picture. Encourage the child to make up a story from looking at the picture.

2. Choose one picture and ask each child in the group to say what they think is happening in the picture.

Activities for Older Children

Pottery

Themes	Our Community, Five Senses, Folk Tales
Goal	To help children experience pottery-making as a form of folk art.
Materials	Potter's clay, small bowls of water, plastic knives, toothpicks, plywood boards or oilcloth.
Description	Cover the table with oilcloth or set out plywood boards for children to work on. Set out clay, carving utensils (knives and toothpicks), and water. Show the children several samples of pottery from other cultures such as Native American pots, Mexican terra-cotta pots, Japanese porcelain bowls, and Dutch delft. Encourage the children to make bowls and pots, carving designs in the sides with the knives and toothpicks.
Variations	1. Invite a potter to come to the class and talk about pottery-making. 2. Read books that include family members making or using clay pots as part of their daily life.

Weaving

Themes	Our Community, Colors, Folk Tales, Clothes We Wear
Goal	To help children experience weaving as a form of folk art.
Materials	Simple loom (cardboard with notches 1/2-inch apart on both ends), yarn.
Description	Talk with the children about how some people tell pictures about their lives in fabric. Some people make quilts, some dye their fabric in bright colors and patterns, some embroider pictures on fabric, and still others weave rugs and wall hangings. Show children samples of weaving, needlework, and quilting. Warp the loom and weave two inches at the top to form a secure edge. Set out the loom and demonstrate how to weave the yarn in-and-out between the threads. Let the children try to follow the in and out sequence. Leave the materials out for a week or two so that children can add to the weaving. Display the weaving along with other samples of weaving and stitchery when finished.
Variations	1. Read the children books about people from other cultures who weave as a part of their daily life. 2. Teach the children how to make an "Ojo de Dios" (Spanish For "Eye of God").

Carving	
Themes	Changes, Alike and Different, Five Senses, Folk Tales, Animals
Goal	To help children explore carving as a form of folk art.
Materials	Sandstone (available at art stores), plastic knives, toothpicks, sample of an Inuit carving.
Description	Tell the children that some people from other cultures enjoy carving things out of stone. Some Inuit artists carve animals out of stone. They pick out a stone and sit with it. They spend time with the stone and get to know it. They listen to the stone and when they know the stone well, they find the shape or animal that the stone wants to become. And then they begin carving the stone into that shape. Show the children pictures of Inuit people carving stone and pictures of their art work. Give each child a piece of sandstone. Encourage them to carry the stone with them all morning. Tell them that after lunch they can carve their stone into any shape they want. Encourage them to listen to their stone. Maybe it will tell them what shape it wants to become.

Masks

Themes
Our Community, Alike and Different, Colors, Folk Tales, Dance and Movement, Holidays and Celebrations

Goal
To help children explore masks as a cultural symbol and art form.

Materials
Poster board cut into circles and ovals, scissors, yarn, feathers, sequins, paint, markers, scrap construction paper, samples of masks, pictures of masks.

Description
Tell the children that people use masks for many different things. Say, "On Halloween we wear masks so that no one will know who we are. Other times people wear masks to keep their faces safe. Masks are also used as part of costumes during special ceremonies and festivals." Discuss how people sometimes act out a story wearing masks. Different cultures or groups of people make and use different kinds of masks. Show the children a variety of masks and encourage them to try them on. Set out the mask-making materials in the art area and encourage children to make their own masks.

Folk Tales

Themes	Our Community, Folk Tales, Books, Families, Holidays and Celebrations, Animals
Goals	To introduce children to the concept of a folk tale.
Materials	Picture books of folk tales, globe or map.
Description	Introduce the concept of folk tales to the children by explaining that folk tales are very old stories. Say, "Grandparents tell their grandchildren these stories. Then the grandchildren grow up and they become mommies and daddies. They tell the same stories to their children. Folk tales help us learn about how our relatives and ancestors lived a long time ago. Every culture has its own folk tales." Hold up the book for the children to see and tell them the title. Show them on the globe or the map where the folk tale came from. Read the story. Leave the books in the book corner for children to look at during free choice time.
Variation	Invite a storyteller to come and share some stories. Ask parents to share the folk tales from their families and their culture.

Folk Music

Themes	Music, Dance and Movement, Holidays and Celebrations, Five Senses, Families
Goal	To introduce children to folk music.
Materials	Collection of records containing folk music from other cultures.
Description	Introduce the concept of folk music to children. Say, "Folk songs are very old songs that were made up by people living a long time ago. We sing them today because they were passed down to our relatives and ancestors. Each culture has its own folk music." Tell them listening to the words of the folk songs helps us learn about how people lived a long time ago. Play a sampling of different kinds of folk songs. Choose one folk song with simple words that children can learn.
Variations	1. Add rhythm instruments and encourage children to keep time with the music. 2. Invite musicians from other cultures to visit the class and perform for the children. 3. Explore lullabies from other cultures.

Special Activities

Children learn from real experiences, whether from meeting real people or exploring real materials. "Trips give adults an opportunity to see for themselves something they have heard or read about. Trips serve not only that same function for children, but also its opposite. They give children an opportunity to see for themselves something they will learn more about later in pictures or books or through conversation" (Redleaf 1983, 3). Walks and field trips offer children firsthand, real-life experiences and are a good starting point for learning about people and different ways of living. These experiences are especially appropriate for children in monocultural programs.

Walks and Field Trips

Here are some ideas for multicultural walks and field trips:

Walks: neighborhood walk
                    house walk
                    people walk

Field Trips: homes of children or staff
                    ethnic grocery stores
                    Third World craft stores

ethnic neighborhoods
neighborhood community centers
ethnic museums and cultural centers
multicultural celebrations or street fairs

Adopt a Classroom

Establish a "sister" relationship with an inner city early childhood education program, a day care center in another part of the state, or a program in another country. Exchange photographs, artwork, and letters. Get together for picnics or other special events.

Invite Visitors

Also consider bringing in special visitors from the community. Parents and family members are the first choice since the children know them on a daily basis. If your program is not multicultural, try contacting the education and outreach volunteer or staff person within local ethnic/cultural associations. Ask visitors to talk about themselves and their family as they live today, rather than speaking on behalf of their people and focusing totally on the past.

Questions to Ponder

1. Which of the unit themes listed in this chapter are already part of your curriculum?
2. Look over the list of unit themes. Which ones might create controversy among the parents? Which ones might work to increase parental support?
3. Review the outline of the curriculum unit on pets. Then choose one theme and create your own curriculum outline emphasizing multicultural concepts and skills.
4. Reflect on the activities and curriculum ideas presented in this chapter. How might your life be different if you had been taught these concepts and skills at an early age?

Resources and References

Baker, Gwendolyn C. *Planning and Organizing for Multicultural Instruction*. Reading, PA: Addison-Wesley, 1983.

Derman-Sparks, Louise. "It Isn't Fair! Anti-Bias Curriculum for Young Children." *Alike and Different: Exploring Our Humanity with Young Children*. Edited by Bonnie Neugebauer. Redmond, WA: Exchange Press, 1987.

Derman-Sparks, Louise. *Anti-Bias Curriculum: Tools for Empowering Young Children*. Washington, DC: NAEYC, 1989.

Forman, George E. and Fleet Hill. *Constructive Play: Applying Piaget in the Preschool.* Menlo Park, CA: Addison-Wesley, 1984.

Kendall, Frances E. *Diversity in the Classroom: A Multicultural Approach to the Education of Young Children.* New York: Teachers College Press, 1983.

Ramsey, Patricia G. *Teaching and Learning in a Diverse World: Multicultural Education for Young Children.* New York: Teachers College Press, 1987.

Texas Department of Human Services. *Culture and Children.* Austin: Texas Department of Human Services, 1985.

Williams, Leslie R., and Yvonne De Gaetano. *Alerta: A Multicultural, Bilingual Approach to Teaching Young Children.* Menlo Park, CA: Addison-Wesley, 1985.

CHAPTER 6

᚜᚜᚜᚜᚜᚜᚜᚜᚜᚜᚜᚜᚜᚜᚜᚜᚜᚜᚜᚜᚜

Holidays and Celebrations

Holidays are special days or times of the year when work is set aside in order to commemorate a special event. Holidays mark many different kinds of events: a religious rite, a great blessing, a terrible sacrifice, the changing seasons, birth and death, the contributions of significant people.

Celebrations evolve within a particular culture or community and reflect the feelings, beliefs, and events that have great meaning in that culture. Celebrations bring people together for a sober purpose or for merriment and fun. It is a time of reconnection with our community, values, and our own individual identity. Holidays give us a chance to express our feelings of joy, sadness, and respect through ceremonies and rituals. Through celebrating, we come together as a group to release our strong feelings. This helps build a sense of community, belonging, and friendship (Texas Department of Human Services 1985).

Holidays in Early Childhood Programs

Holidays, celebrations, and special events are welcomed into the curriculum by children and adults alike. Everyone involved in early childhood programs seems to enjoy the momentary excitement, change in routine, and group spirit that accompanies most holiday celebrations. They are especially enjoyable and important in year-round programs such as day care, where one day tends to run into another with no clearly defined beginning or end. While an enjoyable and even important aspect of human life, we must use care (and caution) when we incorporate holidays and celebrations into our curriculum.

Currently, early childhood education is mirroring the "holiday craze" that has taken over our society. Greeting card companies, paper goods producers, women's magazines, children's television, department stores, and drugstores carry the consumer population through the year going from one holiday to the next. Unfortunately, the curriculum and school supply manufacturers have followed suit. At conventions, teachers line up in droves eager to buy holiday calendar cutouts, holiday bulletin board kits, holiday craft idea packets, holiday ditto sheets, and holiday activity books. Besides filling the curriculum with developmentally inappropriate activities, the yearly calendar is consumed by holiday celebrations. A curriculum plan for the year can end up looking like this:

September:	Fall, Johnny Appleseed, Christopher Columbus
October:	Halloween
November:	Thanksgiving, Food
December:	Christmas, Children Around the World
January:	Winter
February:	Valentine's Day, Friends
March:	St. Patrick's Day, Colors and Shapes
April:	Spring, Easter
May:	May Day, Mother's Day, Flowers and Plants
June:	Father's Day, Summer Fun

This "holiday syndrome" eliminates many developmentally appropriate and more relevant concepts and learning experiences from the curriculum.

Holidays and Multicultural Education

When done well, holidays can be an important and valuable part of the multicultural curriculum. Yet too often the observance of ethnic celebrations and holidays is the only multicultural activity offered all year. I remember when I first became aware of other cultures from teaching in a multicultural/multi-ethnic day care center. At Christmas time I put up a poster of cartoon boys and girls from around the world, each dressed in their country's traditional costume. Throughout the month we made snacks from various cultures and carried out different Christmas observances. We even made Christmas ornaments from different countries. After Christmas, the poster came down and I didn't talk about or explore cultures or differences with the kids again. Yet I was so proud of myself. I really thought that I was doing a good job of providing multicultural education for the children in my class.

Through further teaching experience and reading, I've learned more about holidays and celebrations. Most of the resources on multicultural education warn teachers of the risks involved in focusing on holidays with young children. Holidays have no lasting meaning for children when they are a program's only expression of multicultural education. They are isolated in time and meaning from the rest of the curriculum as well as the children's daily lives. This occurs when teachers, like me, celebrate holidays by making decorations, encouraging the children to dress up in costumes, eat ethnic foods, and listen and dance to ethnic music. When the holiday is over, the decorations come down and life goes back to normal.

Another label for this way of teaching multicultural education is tourist curriculum (see Chapter 2). Children visit a culture by participating in a few activities and then go home to their regular classroom life. This leads to stereotyping and trivializing a culture. As a result, children remember and learn about the exotic characteristics rather than the concept that people live their daily lives differently and that special holidays and celebrations are important events in people's lives.

Holidays Can Teach Negative Values

Focusing on holidays may inadvertently send children the wrong messages. Be aware that by choosing to celebrate certain ones, you risk promoting values that run counter to those you are trying to teach.

Supremacy

Holiday celebrations can emphasize values that conflict with a multicultural curriculum. Many national holidays are ethnocentric. In other words, they promote and encourage the belief that a certain country or a specific group of people is better than another. Columbus Day and Thanksgiving Day can be especially problematic in that they promote the strength, independence, fortitude, and innocence of Europeans while denying the pain, suffering, and destruction of Native Americans.

Materialism

Holidays can be celebrated in a way that promotes consumption of goods and materialism. Sometimes we get the notion that, in order to celebrate a holiday, we must purchase the right clothes to wear for the occasion, the right decorations and adornment, and the right food. For every holiday or special event, there exists a popular prepackaged method of observance. We risk losing the original purpose or method of celebration because of the pressure of television, magazines, and advertising to celebrate in a particular way.

Competition

Teachers also need to be careful that holiday celebrations don't encourage competition and status. Contests that award the child who has the best Halloween costume encourage competition. So do questions and discussions centered around who got the most Halloween candy or who gathered the most candy from the piñata. Valentine's Day ends up focusing on who gave the best Valentine's Day cards, and once again who got the most cards, when the purpose of the holiday is to focus on friendship (Ramsey 1987).

Distorted Thinking

The way in which a holiday is celebrated can encourage distorted thinking in young children. Often holidays are celebrated as if everyone in the world and everyone in our society celebrates the holiday. This simply is not true. Not one holiday is celebrated by everyone. Certainly, everyone does not celebrate religious holidays like Christmas and Easter. Moreover, classroom celebrations should not imply that there is something wrong, lacking, or even bad with people who do not celebrate a particular holiday.

Holidays Can Teach Positive Values

Throughout history, people have celebrated their struggles for freedom, sacrifices for justice, blessings of peace, and the roles of heroes. These celebrations and holidays commemorating various people and national events can provide children with an opportunity to explore concepts of fair and unfair. They can be a time to encourage positive values such as caring for others and taking action against unfair situations in our lives today. We must be sure to teach simple, accurate information and not trivialize events. The Fourth of July is not just a day to have picnics, eat watermelon, and see fireworks. It isn't Picnic Day or Fireworks Day. Rather, it marks the achievement of freedom and independence for a group of people. Martin Luther King's birthday is not just a day to have off, but a celebration of a visionary and the struggle he led.

To Celebrate or Not to Celebrate

Holidays and the decision to celebrate them or not brings up strong feelings for both teachers and parents. I've known many teachers who become outraged with Jehovah Witness families whose children could not participate in the numerous holiday and birthday celebrations. They couldn't understand why the family had to have its child in the program and why they as teachers should be responsible for figuring out what to do with one child during events planned for the entire class. In another center, a group of Jewish parents voiced their concern that the celebration of holidays made them feel unwelcome at the center. With the media and community caught up in celebrating Christmas, they didn't want their children to have to confront and deal with all the holiday hoopla on a daily basis at child care.

These are tough issues. There are no simple answers if we are to take into account each person's beliefs and lifestyles. Questions and concerns over the

celebration of holidays and the participation in celebrations that are not a part of the child's culture must be worked out on an individual basis through open, honest, and thoughtful dialogue (Derman-Sparks 1989).

Some centers seek a quick and simple solution to these often complex and difficult problems. They ban the recognition and celebration of all holidays and celebrations. They see this solution as a way to create a safe, fair, and accepting environment for all of their families. This, however, denies children the knowledge of how other people celebrate events. It creates a situation which can allow children to grow up thinking that the holidays their families celebrate are the only ones in the world, or for a Christian, Euro-American child, that everyone celebrates Christmas and Easter.

Guidelines for Celebrating Holidays

1. Avoid the "holiday syndrome." Don't allow holidays to become the focus of the curriculum (Ramsey 1987).
2. Give all holidays celebrated by the program equal importance (Kendall 1983).
3. Celebrate holidays that are relevant to the children enrolled in the program and seek parent's help in planning accurate celebrations (Texas Department of Human Services 1985).

4. Make children who do not celebrate a particular holiday the welcomed guests at your celebration.

5. Be sensitive to and teach the children that there are groups of people who do not observe Halloween, Christmas, and other similar holidays (Ramsey 1987).

6. Focus on the feelings associated with particular holidays and celebrations rather than the exotic costumes, food, and dances (Ramsey 1987).

7. Celebrate in the context of people and family's daily lives. Point out how each family celebrates in its own way (Derman-Sparks 1989).

8. Give children accurate accounts of historical events and reasons for holiday celebrations (Kendall 1983).

9. Recognize the difference between a celebration and a religious ritual. Do not make a religious ritual into a classroom activity.

10. With young children, don't worry about celebrating holidays on their exact dates. That isn't the focus of the activity, and they won't remember the dates, anyway. Feel free to combine several similar holidays into one celebration (Ramsey 1987).

11. Together with parents plan alternatives ahead of time for the children who cannot participate in a holiday celebration because of religious beliefs.

Ideas for Celebrations

There are many similarities in holidays among cultures. For instance, the theme or focus of many holidays and celebrations is tied to the earth's seasons and to human survival year after year. The way in which people the world over celebrate is also similar. Dancing, cooking and feasting, playing music, and singing are included in many celebrations of merriment. Exchanging best wishes, feelings, thoughts, memories, and gifts between friends and family members is another aspect of observing holidays. Recreating events, remembering the words, thoughts, and work of heroes, is often part of commemorating the birthdays of important people and significant times in a culture's history. Use these similarities to create celebrations and non-religious rituals. Here are some examples adapted from Patricia Ramsey's book, *Teaching and Learning in a Diverse World:*

Units	Concepts
Autumn, Harvest Celebrations	We will have food for the winter, we have worked hard and now reap the rewards.

Units	Concepts
Celebrations of Light, Winter Solstice	The sun warms the cold and is important to us, we need both night and day.
Spring Celebration	Rebirth, replanting, rejoice in the light and warmth.
Summer Celebration, Celebrations of Food	Food is the fruit of the earth, we need water.
Celebrations of the Struggle for Peace, Justice, and Freedom	Fair and unfair, remember the bad times and celebrate the good, keep up the fight.
Celebrations of Fun	Put work aside, play and be silly, celebrate life.
Celebrations of Thanksgiving	Sharing, we are glad for what we have, we are sad for what has happened to Native Americans.
Celebrations of children, mothers, fathers, elders	They are good and do important things, thank you for being who you are.
New Year Celebration	Out with the old and in with the new, another year has passed.

Calendar

Following is a list of many different holidays. Don't try to celebrate them all. Start with incorporating holidays celebrated by the children in your class. Next, carefully consider your curriculum goals. Identify a few holidays that fit into your existing unit themes, and use them to reinforce the concepts and ideals you want to portray to your children. For example, Kwanza reinforces African American pride, pride in one's family, culture, roots in general, and good self-esteem for all children. (Remember, learn about the holiday yourself and always present a holiday or celebration within the context of the curriculum.)

Fall

(The dates of these holidays change each year.)

Rosh Hashanah
Yom Kippur (10 days after Rosh Hashanah)
Hmong New Year Celebration

September

Hispanic Heritage Week (third week)
Good Neighbor Day (fourth Sunday)
8 International Literacy Day
11 Ethiopian New Year
19 World Peace Day
22 Fall begins
27 Native American Day
28 Confucius's Birthday (Japan)

October

Teacher's Day (first Sunday) (USSR)
Universal Children's Day (first Monday)
Columbus Day (second Monday)
2 Mohandas Gandhi's Birthday
8 Hjriat—Moslem New Year
9 Hah'gu Day—Korean Alphabet Day
15 Harvest Home Festival (Canada, England)
15 Sukkoth
16 World Food Day
17 Black Poetry Day
24 United Nations Day
31 Halloween
31 Chinese Chung Yeung Festival

November

Latin American Week (first full week)
National Children's Book Week (third week)
Thanksgiving (fourth Thursday)
National Adoption Week (week of
    Thanksgiving)
3 Culture Day (Japan)
14 Children's Day (India)
15 Shichi-Go-San, Feast of Living
    Children (Japan)
30 Shirley Chisholm's Birthday

Winter

(The dates of these holidays change each year.)

Tu B' Shevat—Festival of Trees
Japanese, Chinese, Korean New Year
Mardi Gras
Chanukah—Jewish Festival of Lights
Ashura
Purim
Holi Bassat Day —Hindu Spring Festival

December

Nine Days Of Posada (third week)
4 Crazy Horse's Birthday
6 St. Nicholas Day (Holland)
8 Mother's Day (Panama)
10 Human Rights Day
13 Sosuharai—Soot Sweeping Day (Japan)
13 St. Lucia Day (Sweden)
21 Winter Solstice
24 Christmas Eve
25 Christmas
25 Children's Day (Congo)
26 Boxing Day (Canada)
26 Family Day (Namibia)
26 Day Of Good Will (South Africa)
26–Jan 1 Kwanza—African American
    Harvest Festival
31 Hogmanay Day (Scotland)

January

Dr. Martin Luther King, Jr.'s Birthday
(third Monday)
1 New Year's Day
2 Ancestry Day (Haiti)
4 Asian Winter festival
5 George Washington Carver Day
8 World Literacy Day
15 Black Christ Festival (Guatemala)
15 Teacher's Day (Venezuela)
15 Seijin-No-Hi—Rite of passage into
    adulthood (Japan)
15 Martin Luther King, Jr.'s Birthday

February

Black History Month
International Friendship Month
President's Day (third Monday)
2 Groundhog Day
8 Narvik Suna Pageant—
    to welcome the sun (Norway)
11 Youth Day (Cameroon)
12 Lincoln's Birthday
14 Valentine's Day
15 Susan B. Anthony's Birthday
22 Washington's Birthday
22 Unity Day (Egypt)
22 Mother's Day (India)
25 Powamo—Hopi Sun Festival
29 Leap Year

Spring
(The dates of these holidays change each year.)
    Passover
    Good Friday
    Easter
    Lazy Bones Day—7 weeks after Easter
        (Holland)

March
    Women's History Month
    Zambia Youth Day (second Saturday)
    Mothering Sunday (last Sunday)
        (United Kingdom)
     3 Hina Matsuri—Japanese Doll Festival
     8 International Women's Day
    17 St. Patrick's Day
    19 Swallow Day—Swallows return to San
        Juan Capistrano
    20 Spring begins
    20, 21, 22 Now-Ruz—New Year (Iran)
    21 International Day for the Elimination
            of Racism
    22 Freedom March at Selma
    28 Teacher's Day (Czechoslovakia)
    29 Taiwan Youth Day
    31 Cesar Chavez's Birthday

April
    Week of the Young Child (first full week)
    Jewish Heritage Week (final week)
     1 April Fool's Day
     2 International Children's Book Day
     5 Arbor Day (Korea)
     8 Buddha's Birthday (Japan, Korea)
     8 Japanese Flower Festival
    17 Children's Protection Day (Japan)
    24 International Youth Day (USSR)
    28 Arbor Day

May
    Native American Indian Month
    Windmill Day (second Saturday)
        (Holland)
    Mother's Day (second Sunday)
     1 May Day
     4 Youth Day (China)
     5 Cinco de Mayo (Mexico)
     5 Kodomo-no-hi—Children's Day
        (Japan)

    18 Peace Day
    19 Youth and Sports Day (Turkey)
    22 Thanksgiving (Haiti)
    19 Malcolm X's Birthday
    24 Education Day (Bulgaria)
    25 African Freedom Day

Summer
(The dates of these holidays change each year.)
    Shavot
    Pentecost

June
    Rose Harvest Festival (first Sunday) (Bulgaria)
    Father's Day (third Sunday)
    Soviet Youth Day (last Sunday)
     1 Harriet Tubman's Birthday
     1 International Children's Protection Day (USSR)
     5 World Environment Day
     8 Muhammad's Birthday
    10 Race Unity Day
    14 Children's Day
    14 Flag Day
    16 Soweto Day—International Day of Solidarity
    (South Africa)
    18 International Peace Day
    20 Summer Solstice

July
    Family Day (first Monday) (Lesotho)
    Heroes Day (first Monday) (Zambia)
    International Cooperation Day (first Saturday)
    (USSR)
    Fisherman's Day (second Saturday) (USSR)
    Unity Day (second Tuesday) (Zambia)
    Girl's Fair (third Sunday) (Romania)
     1 Canada Day
     4 Independence Day
    10 Mary McLeod Bethune's Birthday
    13-15 Festival of Lanterns (Japan)

August
     1 Parent's Day (Zaire)
     6 Hiroshima Day/Peace Festival
     7 Family Day
    11-14 Intertribal Indian Ceremonial
    13 Women's Day (Tunisia)
    15 Harvest Moon Festival (Chinese, Asian)
    26 Women's Equality Day

Questions to Ponder

1. What is your program's policy regarding holiday celebrations?
2. What role do holidays and celebrations play in your program?
3. What changes could you make in how you celebrate holidays with the children?
4. What holidays might you consider eliminating? What holidays could you add?
5. How could you involve parents in the celebration of holidays?

Resources and References

Alternatives. *Alternative Celebrations Catalogue*. 4th ed., Bloomington, IN: Alternatives, 1978.

Derman-Sparks, Louise. *Anti-Bias Curriculum: Tools for Empowering Young Children*. Washington, DC: NAEYC, 1989.

Ramsey, Patricia G. *Teaching and Learning in a Diverse World*. New York: Teachers College Press, 1987.

Texas Department of Human Services. *Culture and Children*. Austin: Texas Department of Human Services, 1985.

CHAPTER 7

╠═╣ ╠═╣ ╠═╣ ╠═╣ ╠═╣ ╠═╣ ╠═╣ ╠═╣ ╠═╣ ╠═╣ ╠═╣ ╠═╣ ╠═╣ ╠═╣ ╠═╣ ╠═╣ ╠═╣ ╠═╣ ╠═╣

Children's Awareness of Differences

Is it hard for you to believe that preschoolers are prejudiced? If so, you aren't alone. Most teachers want to deny the slightest possibility of bias in young children. We think to ourselves, "These children are too young to even notice race much less understand racism." Or we say things like, "Children don't notice differences and besides, they like everyone they meet." There are many indications that young children are aware of differences and form strong attitudes toward themselves and others. This chapter challenges you to look at your assumptions regarding children's awareness of differences and to think about prejudice in new ways.

Differences Children Notice

I wondered if the children in the day care center where I was working noticed any differences. The teachers weren't able to identify many comments from the children to suggest that they were aware of or interested in differences among people. In 1986, I conducted an informal poll of the parents in the center where I was working. Of the parents who completed the questionnaire, 83 percent confirmed that their children were aware of differences, and they described the specific physical attributes their children noticed. Other teachers interested in children's awareness of differences have reported similar results (Derman-Sparks, Higa, and Sparks 1980). The children ages 2 through 5 commented on and asked questions about:

People with Handicaps: wheelchairs, glasses, physical impairments, special facilities.

Gender Differences: male and female anatomy. Some girls said, "I can't be a doctor." "I can't drive a tractor." "I wish I could be a boy because boys can do things girls can't do."

Physical Differences: skin color, facial features, differences in hair color, texture, style.

Cultural Differences: different languages, foreign accents, and celebrations.

Once the results of the parent poll were in, staff had a better idea of what to listen for. As teacher awareness increased, we were able to identify more and more instances where children noticed physical differences and used stereotypes and social labels.

Development of Racial/Cultural Awareness

Development is a continuous, interactive, and cumulative process. We measure this growth in children in terms of years, and it results in accomplishments like learning to walk, talk, and think rationally. Each day we (both adults and children) have experiences and are involved with the people and objects of our social world. We interact with and influence the world and others, and in turn, the world and its people affect us. These ongoing life experiences mesh with our age-related development and this results in an ever-growing sense of self and understanding of the world. This is the nature of human development, and it serves to bring us to ever more complex and more integrated levels of functioning. At any given moment, we are the sum total of our development.

This developmental process can be seen in the progression of children's awareness of and attitude toward human differences. Though development involves the whole child, we often describe growth in terms of specific areas:

physical, intellectual, social, and emotional development. Awareness and understanding of racial and cultural differences is influenced by growth and changes in each of these areas.

For example, in the early years, the development of self-concept and self-esteem play an important role in learning to recognize and accept others. In the preschool years, intellectual development brings the ability to notice how things are different and alike. This mindful attention to detail results in an increasing awareness of how people differ from one another. In the later preschool years and early elementary years, children begin to understand concepts of group membership and physical permanence.

Let's further explore how normal development in the early years contributes to children's awareness of attitudes toward race and culture.

Infancy

The first years of life lay the foundation of self-awareness. Newborn babies notice color contrasts and love to look at human faces. Around four months, they can tell the difference between people who are familiar and people who are strangers, and they respond to and initiate more interaction with people they know. Around six months, babies begin to actively explore people and objects. They may grab your cheek, put their fingers in your mouth, pull on your hair. This is their effort at trying to figure out "what's me and what's not me." In the development of a sense of self, babies progress from noticing human faces to distinguishing between familiar and unfamiliar people, to exploring individuals in order to gain a sense of themselves as an individual.

Infancy is also an important time in the development of feelings and trust in the world. Babies have feelings. They experience fear, anger, sadness, and joy. They learn which feelings are acceptable and which feelings to hide or deny based on how their parents and caregivers respond to them. Adults often deny their children's fear and anger. "There's nothing to be afraid of" is a common response to a child's fear. Older infants and toddlers are often abandoned (put in the crib and left alone) or punished for feeling angry. This lack of acceptance of normal human feelings paves the way for denying and hiding feelings of fear and anger regarding racial differences.

Erik Erikson described the importance of a sense of trust in infancy. Babies need adults and caregivers who will respond to their needs in a loving and timely fashion. By receiving warm, loving, and attentive care, babies learn that the world is a safe place and that people can be counted on and trusted. This is an important step toward believing people are basically good and to letting people into our lives (Erikson 1963).

Toddlers

Sometime between 15 and 18 months, the drive toward self-awareness reaches a high point when children can identify themselves as unique individuals. Now children can really take in all of the messages received about themselves and form a self-concept and self-esteem. Once children fully acquire this sense of self, they are capable of being shamed and of feeling ashamed. Shame is the label for feeling unworthy and defective, like there is something wrong with me because of the way I look, act, think, and feel.

Toddlers are sensitive and "catch" feelings from adults. They pick up on how people feel and will use this information to guide their behavior. If the adult they are with walks into a room and is afraid, children will pick up that fear and act reserved and fearful themselves. If parents or caregivers are uncomfortable, wary, fearful, angry, or warm and accepting around people of other cultures, children will begin to "catch" these feelings and associate them with the situation at hand.

Imitative play emerges during the toddler stage. Children begin to act out simple adult behavior they have observed. Toddlers are most likely to imitate their parents. This comes from wanting to please the adults in their lives and to be "just like mommy" or "just like daddy." They begin to mimic behavior when they copy simple adult acts like talking on the phone, washing dishes, and shaving. During these early years, imitative play becomes more elaborate, and it's common to see preschoolers acting out their home life in the dramatic play area of the classroom. In terms of racial awareness, young children may parrot or mimic their parent's biases in an effort to be like them.

Two Year Olds

The journey toward self-understanding continues as children gain language. Older toddlers and young twos begin using words such as "mine" and "me" to describe themselves. They use the word "you" to describe all others. As their sense of self grows stronger, they go through a period of wanting to be independent and in control of themselves. "No!" "Me do it!" are the commands of a two year old. They need to act on and prove their independence, and children who are not allowed to do things for themselves risk feeling shame. Children who are shamed or develop a shame-based personality may need to put others down in order to convince themselves that they are worthy and acceptable.

Children at this age also begin to define themselves and others by physical characteristics such as skin color, hair color, and anatomy. They notice and are learning the names and location of their body parts. They can classify people by gender. Two year olds are learning the names of colors, and they can distinguish between black and white.

Two year olds may also start using social "labels" rather than skin color to describe another person. For example, when a 2-1/2 year old boy saw an African American man walking across the park he said, "There's a black boy." Later in the day I handed him a black doll. I asked him, "What color is this doll's skin?" He answered, "Black." Then I said, "If the doll's skin is black, what color is its hair?" He looked at the doll for a while and said, "His hair is black." I followed up with, "If its hair is black, then what color is its skin?" He looked again at the doll and got a puzzled look on his face. He looked up at me and then back at the doll. "His skin is brown," he answered. I affirmed, "Yes, its skin is brown and its hair is black." In addition to learning racial labels, children at this age may begin to develop feelings of fear and show discomfort around unfamiliar physical attributes such as facial hair, glasses, skin color, and disabilities.

Threes and Fours

Preschoolers get even better at noticing differences among people. They can name, identify, and match people according to their physical characteristics. By this time, Euro-American children have developed a positive association with the color white and the racial label "white." By age three, minority children are better at classifying faces by color (Aboud 1988). This seems to indicate that children are very aware of their skin color and that minority children have learned more about human diversity than Euro-American children who may believe everyone in the world is like them. Being part of the dominant culture means not having experience with or being aware of minority people living in a society.

Young children are naturally curious about the world. That is why the preschool years are often referred to as the question-asking stage. Preschoolers want to know about themselves and others. At age two their question was "What's 'at?" Now their question is "Why?", which demonstrates their developing interest in the origin and function of things. For example, a four year old may ask, "Where do people get their color? Why are her eyes like that? Am I yellow? What color is my blood?" It is important that young children receive honest, simple answers to their questions because they believe there is an explanation for everything. If they don't know the answer or aren't helped to think about it, they are likely to make up their own distorted answer.

Preschoolers do not understand that objects and people stay the same even though their physical appearance may change. As a result, it is common to hear a boy say, "I'm going to be a mommy when I grow up." Similarly, children may wonder out loud if they will have the same skin color when they grow up, or they may say they want physical features like someone else when they grow up. Children can be helped to understand that many of their features such as their skin color, eye shape, and hair texture are permanent by associating their physical identity with their biological parents.

Young children's thinking is very limited, distorted, and inconsistent, which makes them susceptible to believing stereotypes. For one, they base their thinking on how things look rather than on logical reasoning. They are also very limited in their understanding of time—the past and future have almost no meaning to preschoolers. If they see a Native American on horseback with bows and arrows on television, they may deny that their classmate is a Native American. They may also make false associations between events. For instance, a four year old Euro-American child had an African American teacher. Whenever he saw a black woman walking down the street, he would say, "Look, there's my Wanda." Preschoolers focus on only one aspect of an object at a time. Usually it is a minor detail and they totally miss the main characteristics or the main point of a story. The parents of a four year old came to the center to celebrate their daughter's birthday with her class. These parents recently immigrated from Poland and speak with an accent. In every other way they look, dress, and act like Euro-American parents. But one of the four year olds was afraid and wanted to avoid Katrina's parents because they talked funny.

Fives and Sixes

Children of this age are still into asking questions and trying to make sense of the world. They continue to be interested in physical differences and can easily describe themselves in terms of their own physical features. They are more group-oriented and can begin to understand cultural identity. Fives and sixes will enjoy exploring the cultural heritages of their classmates. They can begin to identify stereotypes as they struggle to discriminate between real and pretend. I was reminded of how important the issue of real and pretend is to young children when I overheard a five-year-old boy repeatedly asking his father, "Dad, is that really real?"

Children at this age can be very rule bound and rigid in their behavior. They like to make rules and will get into conflicts of "fairness." Their understanding of gender and racial behavior may be very rigid and traditional and, as a result, they may tend to choose friends of the same sex and the same race.

Fives and sixes use their increased language ability as their main way of showing aggression. Whereas preschoolers often use hitting to retrieve a toy or to keep a child out of their play, older children use their words to hurt others. They will use insults and call each other names as much as four-fifths of the time. This verbal aggression can be counteracted with discussions of fair and unfair, as this is a moral concept they are able to understand.

Seven to Nine Year Olds

Between the ages of five and seven, children experience a major shift in their thinking. They finally understand that things stay the same even though they may change in appearance. Thus, children realize their gender and skin color will stay the same as they grow into adulthood.

Fully realizing that their culture comes from their family, they add the concept of group membership to their own identity and use it to distinguish themselves from others. Schoolagers can also consider more than one attribute at a time. This allows them to understand that they are a member of a family, an ethnic culture, a classroom, a religion, and a citizen of a town, state, and country.

Schoolagers are very interested in and aware of the world. They want to know what's going on now as well as what happened a long time ago. They can learn about important people and events that have shaped the world.

In terms of emotional development, schoolagers understand the feelings of shame and pride. They are able to talk about and describe these feelings. They develop a true sense of empathy for others, being much more able to put themselves in someone else's shoes.

During the years from seven to twelve, parents and adults will play a major role in helping the child to rethink values and beliefs. Some studies indicate that children's racial attitudes do not change after age nine, unless they experience a major event or major changes in their life (Aboud 1988).

It is critical that we provide chil-

dren with accurate information so that their understanding does not stay like that of preschoolers—distorted and inaccurate. This happens all too often. For example, Marcy Hart, a Native American woman who speaks to groups of elementary school children, is often asked questions such as: "Do the soldiers have to guard the Indians?" "Do the Indians still live on reservations?" "Can they leave the reservation?" "What kind of food do Indians eat?" "Do they grow feathers?" "Do they know how to speak English?" "What kind of clothes do they wear?" "Do they have moms and dads?"

How Prejudice Is Formed

The following discussion focuses on how prejudiced thinking and behavior forms, and highlights the strong connection between prejudice and normal developmental patterns. It is important to remember that these steps in development do not cause prejudice nor do they automatically lead to prejudice. In fact, gaining awareness, learning to identify and classify objects, and forming attitudes about things are positive signs of healthy growth and development.

It's the dominant society and its prevailing values and norms that provide the environment for developing prejudice. Children growing up in a racist society will very naturally learn to classify people the same way as the society at large classifies people. Children quickly learn which skin colors are good and which ones are bad, which ones are privileged and which ones are denied privileges.

Remember, children are not born prejudiced. Prejudice is learned. The developmental process is neutral, and children naturally come to recognize differences. Because society is racist, children pick up the values and beliefs associated with the differences.

Noticing Differences

Infants enter this world alert and aware of their surroundings. As they grow, children notice more and more detail and use all of their senses to take in information from the world around them. Recently, I was holding a six-week-old infant. She was acutely aware of the fact that I was not her mother. I didn't look the same. I didn't talk the same. I smelled different. I held her differently. She began reacting to all of these differences by crying. Because of her age, she didn't have the language ability to put these sensations and perceptions into thoughts or words to label and describe her experience.

As children grow, their perceptual abilities increase and their awareness becomes more and more refined. They naturally notice greater detail. By the age of four, children notice skin color, the shape of eyes, hair color, hair texture, body shape, the way people talk, and how people move their bodies.

There is nothing wrong with developing a greater awareness of differences; it is a very positive and necessary skill.

Identifying and Classifying Attributes

Around age two, children learn to talk and begin using words to express themselves. Language allows them to name and identify all the people and things they've been watching, mouthing, and exploring since infancy. They can label physical characteristics with words: "I'm brown." "My hair is black." "I have blue eyes." That's identification. Two year olds can identify themselves, their own physical characteristics, and the physical attributes of others.

Preschoolers advance beyond identifying objects to sorting them into categories. This is classification. At first, their categories are very simple, as they can only consider one attribute at a time. Young preschoolers enjoy classifying things by color, shape, alike and not alike. Gradually, they learn to distinguish both people and things by their more subtle characteristics and differences. For example, a preschooler may say: "I live on a farm, you live in town." "I live upstairs, you live downstairs." "My hair is blond and your hair is brown." "My skin is white, your skin is brown."

Developing Attitudes and Preferences

The ability to identify and classify is accompanied by the acquisition of attitudes and preferences. Naming, recognizing, and classifying are mental activities that are influenced by cognitive development. An attitude about or a preference for or against something is a response based on a combination of feelings. For children, these feelings result from their efforts to get their needs met—the need to be happy, receive approval, and avoid fear.

The development of a self-concept illustrates the progression from identification to preferences. Self-concept is the knowledge of who I am as a person. Once I can identify myself, I begin the process of learning about who I am. As I get to know myself from experiences in the world and with others, I form attitudes about myself. I may, for example, acquire a positive attitude about my ability to learn and get along with others and form negative feelings about my body and athletic ability. These attitudes influence my behavior: I spend a lot of energy and time with friends, and I avoid sports. If I act on these attitudes long enough, they will become preferences. When describing myself, I may say that I prefer socializing over working out at a gym.

Even very young children begin to make choices and show preferences for people and objects based on the external characteristics they can identify: "I don't want the brown paper, I want the white paper." "I wish I were a boy

because boys can be doctors."

Children show preferences in who they choose as their friends and playmates. Preschoolers exclude playmates with statements like, "You can't play because you have brown skin. You dirty." Remember, these attitudes are influenced by the prevailing social attitudes and values as well as by the child's feelings.

Becoming Prejudiced

Attitudes and preferences become ingrained. As attitudes and preferences grow more rigid, they begin to resemble prejudice. We make choices without thinking about them, acting on an attitude or preference without considering the specific details of a situation. We judge people by their looks without getting to know them as individuals.

Louise Derman-Sparks defines pre-prejudice in children as early thoughts and feelings that can become prejudice. Children can easily develop pre-prejudice because of their limited cognitive understanding, their desire to please adults, or inaccurate information.

The pre-prejudice we see in preschoolers is an emerging behavior pattern of consistently choosing one person over another without rational thinking or reasoning and of automatically disliking people and things that are not familiar or are different.

As adults, we must be careful not to reward or reinforce children's discriminatory behavior. Rather, we want to help children examine their feelings and attitudes and challenge them to accept new information and a variety of people into their lives.

These steps from basic awareness to attitudes and preferences outline normal development as it relates to prejudice. Prejudice is not an inevitable outcome of growth and development, but a hurtful, limiting, distorted behavior learned through experience in a prejudiced society.

Steps in the Development of Prejudice

Awareness — Being alert to, seeing, noticing, and understanding differences among people even though they may never have been described or talked about.

⇓

Identification — Naming, labeling, and classifying people based on physical characteristics that children notice. Verbal identification relieves the stress that comes from being aware of or confused by something that you can't describe or no one else is talking about. Identification is the child's attempt to break the adult silence and make sense of the world.

⇓

Attitude — Thoughts and feelings that become an inclination or opinion toward another person and their way of living in the world.

⇓

Preference — Valuing, favoring, and giving priority to a physical attribute, a person, or lifestyle over another, usually based on similarities and differences.

⇓

Prejudice — Preconceived hostile attitude, opinion, feeling, or action against a person, race, or their way of being in the world without knowing them.

Why Children Are Pre-Prejudiced

There are many reasons why young children exhibit pre-prejudiced behavior. Each of the major child development theories offers a different explanation. Social learning theorists believe that children model or imitate others when they make discriminatory remarks. Behaviorists say that prejudiced behavior is reinforced through the societal stereotypes, values, and attitudes surrounding the child. Freudians or the psychosocial school of thought propose that children act out in discriminatory ways to relieve the anger and painful feelings that come from being humiliated and shamed by the adults in their lives. The cognitivists remind us that while young children create their own ideas, they are immature thinkers likely to confuse the facts and make false assumptions. Thus, while preschoolers are interested in knowing about other people, they are not able to use logical thinking in their preferences for people until they are out of the preoperational stage of development.

Four Explanations for Pre-Prejudiced Behavior

Children as Models
Children imitate the prejudiced comments and behavior they see from their parents, adults, and older children in their lives.

Children as Mirrors
Children's prejudiced behavior and thinking is a reflection of society's values, attitudes, and prevailing stereotypes. They mimic what is seen and heard on TV, read in books, and lived out through institutions.

Children as Victims
Children, who themselves have been shamed and humiliated by adults and older children, transfer their anger and negative feelings onto others who they see as less powerful and less desirable. This is especially true of children living in families with rigid rules and dominating parents who don't allow the child to express feelings of anger, hurt, and sadness.

Children as Limited Thinkers
Cognitive development follows a predictable sequence from simplistic thinking to more complex reasoning. Preschoolers can only understand the world and other people from their own experience and are likely to confuse the facts and focus on irrelevant details. Young children reach false conclusions about the world because they build their own beliefs by making incorrect associations between events and ideas.

None of these explanations provide a complete explanation of pre-prejudice. But each perspective provides a partial answer limited by the aspect of behavior it focuses on. As early childhood educators, we know that it is important to look at children's behavior from several different angles. In real life, a person interacts with family, friends, neighbors, schools, and the community. Just as our lives are made up of a combination of relationships and interactions, it is likely that in reality each of these perspectives on pre-prejudice interact with one another. When thinking about the origins of prejudice you can combine the explanations to provide a comprehensive understanding of young children's prejudiced behavior.

Stereotypes Commonly Accepted by Young Children

Children's limited experience and distorted thinking make them highly susceptible to stereotypic thinking. Following is a list of stereotypes young children are likely to believe.

Asians	all look alike
	have yellow skin
	have slanty eyes and can't see very well
	are polite and bow when they greet people
	do karate
	celebrate exotic festivals
Africans	live in huts and don't wear much clothing
	live in the jungle with wild animals
African-Americans	have funny hair
	get in a lot of fights
	all look alike
Native Americans	take scalps
	have red skin
	use tipis as houses
	speak in grunts
	wear feathers and costumes
	ride horses
	don't live now
Hispanics	have only brown hair and brown eyes
	are greasy and unclean
	have piñatas at all their parties

Adapted from Kathleen McGinnis, *Cultural Pluralism in Early Childhood Education*, 1979, p. 5-8.

Effects of Prejudice on Euro-American Children

Growing up in a segregated, racist, and prejudiced society influences children's development. This is especially true in the areas of self-esteem and self-concept. It is important to realize that prejudice affects Euro-American children and minority children differently. The development of Euro-American children is influenced by bias in at least four ways.

Denial of Reality

Children learn to see but not acknowledge the differences between people. This is because, time after time, children's honest questions and comments about people are met with responses meant to silence them: "Shhh." "Don't say that." "It's not nice to stare." "Don't be rude." "We don't talk about those things in public." Sensing adults' uneasiness with talking about physical differences and receiving criticism from noticing the differences, children gradually become silent. They stop asking about people and other cultures. This whole process stunts children's normal growth in terms of noticing, identifying, and classifying differences. Children learn to adopt

the dominant society's denial of human uniqueness: "We are all the same." "It doesn't matter what color you are." "We are all the same on the inside."

The lack of representation of people of color in government, the media, and high status professions, along with the lack of integration in communities, neighborhoods, and schools create a false reality. As a result children can grow up thinking that the world is made up only of white Euro-Americans.

One Right Way

Children's thinking is influenced by growing up in a prejudiced society. When we raise children in a segregated, biased environment they grow up believing that their way of living in the world is the one and only right way. There is one correct way to be a family, one appropriate language to speak, one right religious faith to practice. This type of thinking closes children off from learning about and being able to live side-by-side with those who are different from them. In addition, this thinking produces judgmental attitudes, resulting in the stance that people who live differently, speak differently, practice different religions, and live in countries that make decisions differently are not only wrong—they are bad.

Superiority

Prejudice influences the development of children's self-esteem. Ideally we hope that children experience an inner sense of goodness about themselves as worthwhile, capable, lovable human beings. Too often, children's inner sense of self is lacking. They try to protect themselves and build their sense of self by focusing on external factors such as what they have or what they can do. To a certain extent, Euro-American children's sense of self-esteem comes from believing that they are better than anyone else. Euro-American children may secretly tell themselves, "I can feel good about myself as long as I know you (people of color) aren't as good as me." As a result, we find Euro-Americans needing to criticize, ridicule, and reject people who are different in order to maintain their own sense of self worth.

Fear and Hate

When children are raised in a society that is biased against people of other races, cultures, and lifestyles, they learn to hate and fear people who are different from them. Some people deal with their fear of others through avoidance. For example, a Euro-American who is afraid of African Americans may not drive into a predominantly Black neighborhood. Other people deal with their fears by putting up a defense of anger. They act out their fear of differences in angry and hurtful ways, like participating in or condoning racial violence. This fear and hatred of others can also be seen in the irrational thinking of Euro-Americans that, if people of color gain success, white people will be taken over, dominated by the minority groups, and life as we know it will end.

Effects of Prejudice on Children of Color

Prejudice seems to affect children of color differently than Euro-American children. That's because the dominant Euro-American culture bombards minority children with messages about their place in society, their values to society, and how they should behave.

This section highlights recent studies related to children and prejudice. The vast majority of these studies focused on Euro-American and African American children. Though fewer studies have focused on Hispanic, Asian, and Native American children, they have tended to produce similar findings.

Self-Esteem

Children of color receive messages from their own culture about their goodness, beauty, and strength. They are taught to be proud of their racial and ethnic heritage. Janice Hale-Benson describes how African American families build self-esteem in their children:

> Black parents have been challenged to foster positive self-concept development in their children. They bolster their children's ego by such comments as, "You're just as good as anybody else." They must soothe the anxieties that arise in their children when they engage in competition or social comparison with white children (Hale 1986, 64).

Contrary to popular belief, there is no evidence of low self-esteem in young minority children. Their self-esteem is as equally high as that of Euro-American children, but whereas Euro-American children's self-esteem is related to ethnic attitudes, this does not seem to be the case with children of color.

Group Identity

Earlier in this chapter I told a story about a two-year-old Euro-American boy who called both an African-American man and a brown-skinned doll "black." He was using the social label before he could clearly distinguish similarities and differences between himself and others. Euro-American children tend to learn and use ethnic or racial labels at an extremely young age before they can intellectually classify alike and different. Minority children learn and use labels as a second step in self-identification. The use of labels results from noticing similarities and differences (Aboud 1988).

Both children of color and Euro-American children begin to form attitudes around the same age. Many researchers have observed children's doll play and questioned children about their doll preference. Euro-American children almost always choose the white doll, illustrating a strong pro-white attitude that remains constant throughout childhood.

Many African-American children choose the white dolls rather than the black doll. This suggests that children of color do not express a high attachment to their own ethnic group during the preschool years. Another study of Hispanic children illustrates this aspect of ethnic identity and sheds light on a possible explanation for minority children's identification with the dominant culture:

> Children of 4 and 5 years of age who did not yet attend school preferred the Hispanic doll (75 percent) whereas those who attended school preferred the White doll (85 percent). The former group presumably had little exposure to Whites because they lived in a homogeneous neighborhood, whereas the latter were interacting daily with White teachers (Aboud 1988, 42).

Many interpretations are possible for why many minority children prefer to play with white dolls. It may be that the child wants to please the adult watching or questioning them. Or it may be that the child has picked up messages that being white is better.

Frances Aboud, author of *Children and Prejudice,* explains this characteristic in terms of children's emotions and motivations. Young children's awareness of differences is based primarily on emotions such as fear and happiness. Children are afraid of adult disapproval and actively seek adult approval for their actions. Aboud suggests that minority children may have a high need for approval because they see Euro-Americans getting more approval.

Around age five or six, minority children correctly identify their own ethnicity, and by age seven, children of color demonstrate more attachment to their own ethnic group. It isn't until ages eleven or twelve that minority children become fully aware of social classifications and their ethnic group's place within society.

Attitude Toward Others

Whereas Euro-American children begin to form negative attitudes about people who are different from them around three or four, and they develop a fairly high level of rejection of other ethnic groups that remains consistent until at least age seven, we know that young minority children have positive feelings toward and may even identify with Euro-Americans. This doesn't change once they become attached to their own ethnic group. "When Black children adopt a preference for Blacks, their attitude toward Whites does not necessarily become rejecting" (Aboud 1988, 41). It isn't until sometime after the age of seven that minority children develop negative attitudes toward other ethnic groups.

Interracial Children's Identity

Developing a sense of identity can be especially confusing to young children with a multiracial background. For example, a child in your classroom might be both Hispanic and Asian, or both Euro-American and African American. Some minority children, too, have been adopted into white families. Like all preschoolers, they are recognizing differences and developing classification skills. Questions such as "Who am I?" and "What am I?" are especially important to (and difficult for) them. Francis Wardle reminds us that interracial children are the sum total of their ethnic heritage. To ensure positive self-development, we as early childhood teachers must embrace, acknowledge, and celebrate all of the richness that interracial children bring to our classrooms. We do them an injustice when we try to put them into neat little categories. It is especially harmful to identify an interracial child by one culture or associate the child with the parent of color. We must help interracial children feel good about their physical features and their families. Most of all, we must accept and recognize each interracial child as a unique individual (Wardle 1987).

Questions to Ponder

1. What physical characteristics do your students notice or talk about?
2. When did you first become aware of your racial and ethnic identity?
3. When did you become aware of other racial/ethnic groups?
4. How has growing up in American society influenced your awareness of and attitude toward people who are racially/ethnically different from you?

Resources and References

Aboud, Frances. *Children and Prejudice*. New York: Basil Blackwill, 1988.

Anselmo, Sandra. *Early Childhood Development*. Columbus: Merrill, 1987.

Derman-Sparks, Louise. *Anti-Bias Curriculum*. Washington, DC: NAEYC, 1989.

Derman-Sparks, Louise, Carol Tanaka Higa, and Bill Sparks. "Children, Race, and Racism: How Race Awareness Develops," *Interracial Books for Children Bulletin*. Vol. 11, No. 3 and 4. New York: Council on Interracial Books for Children, 1989.

Edwards, Carolyn Pope. *Promoting Social and Moral Development in Young Children: Creative Approaches for the Classroom*. New York: Teachers College Press, 1986.

Erikson, Erik. *Childhood and Society*. New York: W. W. Norton & Co. Inc., 1963.

Hale - Benson, Janice E. *Black Children. Their Roots, Culture and Learning Styles*. Baltimore: John Hopkins University Press, 1986.

Hendrick, Joanne. *Total Learning: Developmental Curriculum for the Young Child*. 3rd ed. Columbus: Merrill, 1990.

McGinnis, Kathleen. *Cultural Pluralism in Early Childhood Education*. St. Louis: Parish Board of Education, Lutheran Church, Missouri Synod, 1986.

Morrison, George S. *The World of Child Development*. Albany: Delmar, 1990.

Phillips, Carol Brunson. "Foreword," *Alike and Different: Exploring Our Humanity with Young Children*. Edited by Bonnie Neugebauer. Redmond, WA: Exchange Press, 1987.

Seifert, Kelvin L., and Robert J. Hoffnug. *Child and Adolescent Development*. Boston: Houghton Mifflin, 1987.

Pulaski, Mary Ann Spenser. *Your Baby's Mind and How It Grows*. New York: Harper and Row, 1978.

Singer, Dorothy G., and Tracey A. Revenson. *A Piaget Primer: How A Child Thinks*. New York: Plume Books, 1978.

Wardle, Francis. "Building Positive Images: Interracial Children and their Families," *Alike and Different: Exploring Our Humanity with Children*. Edited by Bonnie Neugebauer. Redmond, WA: Exchange Press Inc., 1987.

CHAPTER 8

⌐⌐⌐⌐⌐⌐⌐⌐⌐⌐⌐⌐⌐⌐⌐⌐⌐⌐⌐⌐⌐⌐⌐⌐⌐⌐

Culturally Responsive Care and Education

"Day care centers must be viewed as critically important cultural settings that bend fragile twigs and leave a mark on the great oak trees of future generations."
—Darla Ferris Miller

Have you ever been frustrated by or found yourself wondering about:
- a child who refuses to play by himself and interrupts other children who are playing quietly and independently?
- a child who has difficulty choosing an activity and prefers to cling to you, her teacher?
- a child who asks for your help or attention by verbally teasing you?
- a child who resists looking you in the eye when you are reprimanding him?
- a child who has a high energy level and turns every activity into a large motor experience?
- a child who goes limp and becomes silent when you directly confront her behavior?
- a baby who prefers to be held and gently rocked, and who cries loudly whenever you put him on the floor to play?
- a three year old who drinks from a bottle and can't go to sleep without a pacifier in her mouth?
- a child who comes to school every day in "party" clothes and his parents warn him to stay away from paint and other messy activities?
- a parent who is very angry because her daughter comes home with a dirty face and sand in her hair?
- a child who enjoys lively play with one or two playmates, but is silent and hangs back in group activities?

Differences between children and teachers or parents and teachers often cause problems. Teachers must realize that these differences may be a result of culture. Culture influences how families raise children and how a child behaves, communicates, and learns. These behavior patterns and childrearing practices reflect a specific culture's history, values, beliefs, and current situation.

This chapter will help you cope with the differences that influence your classroom by identifying ways in which culture and family patterns mold the children you serve. Often family studies is not part of an early childhood teacher's training program. This chapter provides you with some basic information about families and practical ideas for providing culturally responsive child care. As you read through this material, look inward and gain insight into your own culture. Reflect on your own family experiences. Think about how your orientation toward family may affect your work with children and families.

Take Time to Look at Families

Is a family a mommy at home with the baby and a daddy at work? Is it grandmas, grandpas, aunts, and uncles? Is it celebrating holidays, graduations, funerals, weddings, and births? Government defines family for the census. Dictionaries define family. In terms of multicultural education for young children, it is important to realize that your own definition of family relates to your ethnicity, economic class, and life experience. For this discussion we will define family as a group of people with a long-term commitment to one another who share living space and the tasks involved in maintaining the group.

Let Go of the Myth

The traditional or nuclear family is actually the white middle class Euro-American model of family. When we think of family we imagine a two-parent family with two children, a boy and a girl. They own their own home, two cars, and a dog. The father works full-time outside the home to support the family. The mother stays home raising the children, providing them with wonderful experiences and preparing nutritious meals. Focusing on this image make us feel warm, safe, and secure. In reality, 86 percent of families living in the western culture fall outside of these traditional family patterns. Other kinds of families include single-parent families, dual career families, lesbian and gay families, blended families, and families that live communally. Early childhood professionals need to look beyond the idea of the traditional family as the one "right," "correct," or "normal" family model in order to see the unique characteristics and strengths of all families.

Recognize that Families Transmit Culture

Families pass their culture on to their children through a process known as *enculturation*. In other words, families socialize their children to become members and participate in a particular culture. Though the family lives in the United States, it may function within a subculture based on its ethnicity and/or economic class. Children are first socialized into their particular subculture (in this case ethnic group) so that the child's first experience with the values, beliefs, and ways of the Euro-American culture come with participation in day care or an early childhood education program.

Cultural values change over time. A family's cultural values may change from one generation to the next depending on how long the family has lived in the United States. A refugee family, struggling to adapt to an entirely different culture, will find strength and support from the familiarity of their native language and traditional practices. A sec-

ond generation family may be bilingual, functioning successfully in the dominant society while continuing to live out its ethnic practices at home. Often the ability to read, write, and speak the native language is lost by the third generation but strong evidence suggests that ethnic values, identification, lifestyle, and behavior are retained through the second, third, and fourth generations after immigration (McGoldrick, Pearce, Giordano 1982).

Families also differ in their desire to become like the traditional American family. Families who are in this country for a brief period of time because of schooling or a work opportunity may want their children to "experience American life" and learn some English, but do not want their child to lose their native language and customs. Other families may be quite new to the United States but plan to stay here permanently. They may want their child to learn English quickly and to actively participate in "American" holidays and celebrations. They may be concerned that their accent will cause their child to stand out and not be accepted by other children. In recent years many families have come to this country as refugees. They have been forced to leave behind their homeland, lifestyle, and extended family. While they may want to learn English and how to live in this culture, their own traditions and language provide a great feeling of security as they go through a time of many changes.

Culture Influences Childrearing Patterns

Culture influences childrearing and as a result, people from different cultural backgrounds have differing ideas about what constitutes quality child care. According to Darla Miller:

> Methods of caring for and educating young children routinely expected by high-income families may shock and repel low-income families—and visa versa. Routines considered desirable by one group may be seen as inane by another. Guidance strategies believed in some cultural settings to be essential to healthy growth may be considered inhumane and destructive in others. What some consider to be essential experiences for effective early learning, others consider utter nonsense. Social workers, early educators, and child care professionals have often felt the tension among these opposing views and have sometimes been snagged unknowingly by their own culturally biased assumptions (Miller 1989, 2).

In reality, culture influences how a parent responds to all elements of childrearing such as:

age-related expectations of children
interest in and concern over children acquiring skills by a certain age
sleep patterns and bedtime routines
children's role and responsibility in the family
toilet training
diet and mealtime behavior
discipline and child guidance methods
how parents talk to children
how parents show affection
importance of gender identity and traditional sex roles
dress and hair care
illness and use of medicine or folk cures and remedies
use of supplementary child care
acceptance, meaning of, and response to crying
child's attachment to adults, separation from adults

Culture Influences the Classroom

As a teacher, you have your own culturally-based beliefs about how each of these childrearing issues should be handled in your classroom, as well as by parents at home. Sometimes we view our own style of childrearing as the right way. Remember, each culture successfully raises new generations of children according to their own values and beliefs. We must be willing to look at children's and families' life experiences without placing judgment.

Early childhood programs institute policies and procedures that define a specific style of child care and education. A program can never be multicultural if its staff expects one style of child care to compliment the endless variety of childrearing patterns. Conflicts arise when programs rigidly follow one style. Parents and teachers may disagree about what's best for a child. A teacher may think she clashes with a child because of "personality" issues, when in fact it is a difference in culture. You have probably observed or at least sensed these types of conflicts.

On the following pages is a diverse list of culturally based family patterns, childrearing practices, and values, all of which may influence your classroom. Use this list to help you name sources of conflict, recognize the child's experience, and understand the parent's perspective. The right-hand column offers suggestions for alternative teaching practices and attitudes. Use this list to develop and institute culturally responsive child care.

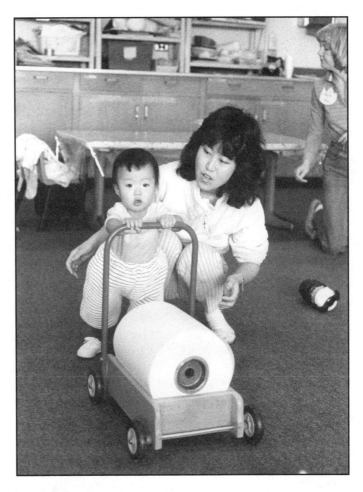

Culture and the Classroom

Cultural Standard	Child's Experience	Classroom Strategy
Family System		
Highly mobile, nuclear	Child has little contact with extended family; friends take the place of extended family.	Sponsor family events to help families build support systems, encourage child's friendships to continue away from school.
Clan network in which family units live in the same neighborhood or community	Child is used to a high level of activity within the home, with people coming and going (dropping by). Child may regularly eat or sleep in more than one household.	Child may become bored if there is little activity. Provide opportunities to move freely around room. Thrives on free choice play. Provide activities that utilize cooperation and sharing.
Extended family that lives together and shares resources	Child is involved in all activities and is used to a high level of cooperation and responsibility. Separating children can be seen as breaking up family.	Child may try to watch out for younger brothers and sisters. Consider mixed age groups that allow siblings to stay together or allow child to "visit" sibling during the day. Provide activities that build cooperation and sharing. Understand that family may not need or attend family-oriented center events.
Power Structure		
Democratic family with members sharing in decision making	Child is allowed/encouraged to negotiate, compromise.	Offer child real choices; use problem solving techniques.
One family member has the power and authority to make decisions	Child is expected to obey, follow commands, respect adult authority.	Child may resist making activity choices and may be uncomfortable looking adults in the eye or calling them by name. Don't insist on eye contact; be aware child may need your help in making choices. If a concern exists, try to connect with the powerful adult family member.

Cultural Standard	Child's Experience	Classroom Strategy
Work/Employment		
Career-oriented; job is very rewarding; parent brings work home and has few other interests	Parent wants child to have similar opportunities to be creative and develop own interests; child relates to learning through play.	Provide meaningful choices; opportunities for creativity and self-expression.
Boring, monotonous job or a job that requires little initiative or autonomy. Personal fulfillment comes from recreation	Parent doesn't expect child to enjoy learning; models attitude of work now and play later; may expect child to sit through long lessons.	Guide child in free play if he tends to become wild. Encourage and demonstrate short, quiet breaks from long lessons.
Attitudes Toward Day Care		
Day care is a public place and the teacher should be respected	Child comes to school in dress clothes, is told to obey the teacher, and may not call the teacher by her first name.	Provide smocks that actually cover and protect clothing. Respect child's need to be submissive and speak to you formally. Consider adding a title (Ms., Mrs. or Mr.) if you use your first name.
Day care is for the child, part of a modern extended family network	The child may come in worn, casual play clothes. The child and parent call teachers by her first name.	Don't be offended or judge the child based on her clothes. Consider allowing the child to call you by your first name.
Child Development		
Infancy equals the first twelve months of life	Child is breast fed for the first six to twelve months. Discipline begins with saying "no" and slapping the child's hand, and letting child cry after six months of age.	You may feel that the child's parent is pushing the child. Use active listening techniques and simple commands toward the end of the first year.
Infancy equals the first two years of life	Child is breast fed for the first two years; may spend all of waking hours with mother and sleep with mother. Few demands on child at this time. Toilet training is gradual. Child is not pushed to learn self-help skills.	Recognize that this child may have a difficult adjustment to child care due to grieving the perceived loss of mother. Find ways to hold and carry this child. Do not force him to play alone for long periods.

Cultural Standard	Child's Experience	Classroom Strategy
Infancy equals the first five years of life	Child is breast fed for the first two to four years or is allowed to have a bottle for the first five years. Toilet training is gradual. Discipline begins at the end of this period. Parent may not be concerned about developmental milestones.	Accept what may look like delayed separation anxiety. It may peak during preschool years and catch you off guard. Allow child to have transitional objects such as stuffed animals or blankets. Push developmental information on parent only if you have a strong concern about delays.

Social Experiences

Cultural Standard	Child's Experience	Classroom Strategy
Parents experience discrimination, lack of opportunities, violence and police hostility	Child's demands are ignored or ridiculed as child is prepared to survive in a hostile environment, taught to tolerate unfairness, and not to expect too much.	Delay your response to a child. Respect parent's need to keep child safe. Use firm discipline.
Parent experiences privilege, many opportunities, and lives in a safe environment	Child is given what she wants, taught to expect her needs will be met and that the world is a safe place.	Consider granting parent's request for individual treatment of child.

Values

Cultural Standard	Child's Experience	Classroom Strategy
Strong, close-knit family	Child taught that the family comes before the individual. Members are expected to sacrifice personal desire for the family.	Recognize child may be expected to miss school in order to take care of a family member.
Interpersonal relationships	Infant usually in the company of others and is held most of the time. Child is people-oriented.	Find ways to hold and carry infant. Provide lots of touching and caressing. Play "people" games like peek-a-boo. Understand that child may be more interested in playmates than in manipulating toys and objects. Use eye contact to guide child's behavior.
Independence	Infant only held for feeding, comforting, and moving from place to place. Child sleeps alone for long periods of time, Child has own space and toys at home.	Recognize parent's fear that too much holding and cuddling will "spoil" the baby. Allow infant to play on the floor and children to move independently around room, bring own toys from home; minimize sharing.

Cultural Standard	Child's Experience	Classroom Strategy
Present-time oriented rather than past- or future-oriented	Child's lifestyle is very process-oriented; little emphasis on routines and eating or sleeping by the clock.	Offer flexibility in arrival and departure. Avoid threats and bribes to get child to eat or nap.
Cleanliness	Infant may be spoon-fed, child's face is washed often, clothes are kept clean, and toilet training may begin after the first year.	Keep the child's face clean. Avoid getting sand in the child's hair. Put the child in clean clothes before going home from day care.
Honor, dignity, and pride	By their behavior and achievement, child upholds family honor. Child disciplined for rude behavior and poor manners.	Share child's achievements with parent. Help child to learn manners. Be sensitive to parent's need to maintain pride and dignity when confronting parent about child's negative behavior.
Personalism—the inner person is more important than outer achievements.	Each child is accepted as an individual. Child is not pushed to reach developmental milestones or learn self-help skills early. Parent may trust individual teacher more than the program.	Avoid motivating child through competition. Understand that child may be more interested in friends or helping the teacher than in completing tasks. Avoid misreading parent's acceptance of child's abilities as lack of interest.
Modesty	Child taught to keep a low profile in public and discouraged from drawing attention to herself; it is not acceptable for child to ask for what she wants. There may be little public display of affection.	Respond to child's cries promptly. Don't allow this child to become an invisible member of your class. This child may not ask much of you and easily can go unnoticed. Avoid forcing the child to talk during group time.

Styles of Communication

Self-expression	Child taught to express personality through verbal communication; is praised for speaking and listening well.	Look for child to enjoy group time and creative expression, and engage the adults in verbal interplay; try teaching through dramatics, stories, and songs.

Cultural Standard	Child's Experience	Classroom Strategy
Strong oral tradition	Culture passed down through storytelling, poetry, and song. Adults guide child's behavior by telling a story with a moral.	Recognize teachable moments for telling a story to motivate or challenge the child's behavior; also use lullabies and songs.
Expressing feelings is permitted.	Child is allowed to cry, scream and have temper tantrums.	Accept child's crying while comforting the child. Stay with child when he is having a temper tantrum.
Feelings should be hidden	Crying and screaming are discouraged.	Pick up infant as soon as she cries. Try ignoring outbursts, or remove child from group to express feelings.

Child Discipline

Cultural Standard	Child's Experience	Classroom Strategy
Harsh; spanking, threats, and verbal humiliation	Child learns to respect authority and to come the first time he is called.	Child may ignore or not take positive discipline techniques seriously. Try using firm statements and commands, humor, gentle harassment and animated gestures.
Motivate child toward inherent goodness	Child is given freedom to explore consequences. Adults talk in quiet voices and warn child of possible embarrassment as a result of misbehavior.	Child may go limp or show other signs of passive resistance if you discipline him too strongly. Use natural consequences; ask rather than command; and talk softly.
Motivate child toward good behavior	Child is disciplined by scolding, threats and promises.	Try modeling desired behavior using "if then" statements: "If you put the toys away, then you can go outside." Praise good manners and polite behavior.
Reduce conflicts and foster harmony	Child is scolded, shamed, and humiliated for fighting or having a temper tantrum.	Try talking to the child in a low, hushed voice. Praise cooperation.

Culture Creates Dilemmas in the Classroom

When I was a director of a white, suburban, middle-class child care center, I enrolled a rather large three-year-old boy whose family had just come from Israel to spend one year in the United States. The little boy arrived for his first day of school complete with a baby bottle full of chocolate milk in one hand and a pacifier in the other. The teaching staff was appalled by such parenting practices, and the teachers of the three year olds were bound and determined to stick to their rule of "no bottles" and "no pacifiers." This was a preschool room—not a toddler room, for heaven's sake. The little boy screamed, kicked, and cried as soon as he entered the room. He did this every day, all day for almost a month. He became the topic of conversation in the staff lounge, the center kitchen, the playground, and the hallway.

Every staff person had a different complaint about this child. He cried too much. He was too immature. He was spoiled. He wasn't ready for day care. His parents were lazy because they hadn't weaned him from the bottle or pacifier. His parents were spoiling him. His parents must be ignorant—didn't they know about baby bottle syndrome? One teacher was panicked that soon all of the three year olds would be begging—no, demanding—their own bottle of chocolate milk. The more staff complained the less interested they became in a solution. They thought this little boy was bad. The parents were bad. It was a bad and hopeless situation, and they wanted me to kick him out. From the child care training I do today, I know that this happens all of the time.

In dealing with cultural dilemmas such as this, I offer these suggestions:

1. Analyze the situation and identify ways in which you may be involved in a cultural dilemma. Ask yourself, "What is the child's experience at home?" and "How is the child's experience related to a cultural practice or value?" In this case, the teachers and parents had different goals for the child based on cultural values regarding specifically, when does a baby stop being a baby? From the parent's perspective, their son was still a baby. From the teacher's cultural perspective, he was a preschooler.

2. Don't blame the child. The child is not bad, evil, spoiled, or developmentally delayed. Contrary to how it may seem, the child is not out to get you. The child may be acting in a culturally appropriate way. The little boy in my story was an absolute delight to his parents.

3. Get information. Go to the child's file and read through the enrollment forms. Call the parent and set up a time to talk. Find out what the behavior means to the parent, what the parent would do in this situation, and what has been done in the past.

4. Realize the child can't cope. He is responding to a new situation in the ways he knows how. His only expectation is to receive care that is similar to what he has known his whole life. These big changes are scary, frustrating, and angering. The boy in our story found himself separated from his parents and in the company of people who spoke a different language. He was totally overwhelmed. That bottle was his only form of security.

5. Respond to the child and parent as individuals. Culturally responsive caregiving and education means the willingness to bend, change, and revise in order to meet individual needs. It may mean breaking the rules, making exceptions to the rules, or changing the rules in order to provide complimentary care and culturally appropriate education.

Early Childhood Programs as Extended Family

When working with young children, we cannot separate the child from the family. Early childhood teachers must broaden the vision of their mission to encompass serving families, not just children. Teachers in high quality programs realize this, and they seek to foster the child's development and education while at the same time supporting parents in creating a healthy, satisfying family life.

Often families reach out to child care and nursery school programs to supplement the care and education received from the family. In this sense, early childhood programs come to resemble an extended family. Early childhood programs become part of the extended family network by accepting all types of families, establishing respectful parent-teacher relationships, and including parents in all aspects of the program.

Make Complementary Care Your Goal

The early childhood program also introduces the child to new ways of eating meals, talking to one another, celebrating special events, and getting along with people. In this sense, each early childhood program has its own culture that it passes on to the children enrolled.

Children, however, experience conflict and confusion when they live out one set of values at school and another set of values at home. A teacher may expect children to behave one way and the parents expect their child to behave in an opposite way. For example, a child is caught in the middle when a teacher wants him to ask for the toy that he wants to play with and his native culture teaches him that it is selfish to ask for what he wants.

Early childhood programs must be sensitive and responsive to all the different ways families raise children. As an extension of the family, programs must make every attempt to provide care and education that matches and enhances the child's family life.

Confusing, contradictory messages about themselves, their parents, or their families can only hurt a young child's self-concept and ethnic identity: "Remember what happened to E.T. when he got too far from home? He lost his power over the world. And so it is with our children when their school settings are so different from home that they represent an alien culture to them. They too lose their power" (Phillips 1988, 47).

Accept Differences

As a teacher, you may be tempted to negatively evaluate the families you serve. Perhaps this comes from lack of awareness or experience. Maybe you didn't realize that families could be so different from one another and still be successful at childrearing. Perhaps when confronted by the differences, you responded out of your own experience with questions and comments such as: "Doesn't everyone do this?" "I didn't know that everyone doesn't do what I do," and "I didn't know that other people do that." As professionals working with families with young children, we need to emerge from our own cultural isolation and realize that "No, everyone doesn't do it my way."

Involve Families in Your Program

When families participate in early childhood programs, they open up their family system to include other adults in the caring for and teaching of their youngest members, the children. In this way, early childhood programs are like extended families, and they share in the responsibility for encouraging racial and ethnic awareness. As an extended family member, programs must provide care and education in a way that complements each family that they serve.

As early childhood educators, we talk about individualizing curriculum and the importance of matching activities and experiences to the needs, interests, and abilities of each child. This is individualized planning at the classroom level. How can we individualize care and service to families? How can a program meet the wants and needs of each family?

One way to make sure that your center's multicultural program meets family's needs is to get to know each family, provide ongoing communication about multicultural events, and include parents at all levels of planning.

Enrollment Meeting

Intake is the perfect time to establish a relationship with the parents and children. It is very important that staff make parents feel welcome and accepted. A personal relationship with parents gives a much stronger message than the written information in the program brochure or parent handbook. This is the time to tap into parents' knowledge of their children and to ask them to share information about their family's beliefs and practices. Inform parents of the center's commitment to a multicultural program. Reiterate that commitment by describing the center's multicultural education program in the center's brochure and parent handbook. Conclude the intake interview by inviting the parents to participate and share their family's traditions with their children's classes.

Enrollment forms can be used to collect information about a family's culture and its influence on parenting and family life. Some people may feel that asking such questions is invading the privacy of others. The truth is that parents feel valued and can be confident that center staff won't overlook or forget this important information when it is included on the enrollment forms. In addition, teachers need complete and accurate information if they are to meet the individual needs of each child. Use the information gathered on the enrollment forms to individualize caregiving styles and routines and to plan curriculum activities, celebrations, and family events. Respecting and including cultural information in the daily life of the program tells families that you respect them and will help them preserve their language, values, and traditions. Here are some questions to include in your enrollment forms or in the intake interview:

Family Structure
- How many children are in your family?
- Do any members of your extended family live with you? Please name them.
- Who else has cared for your child?
- What type of residence do you live in?

Parenting

- What words does your child use for urination? bowel movement?
- Describe your child's eating schedule.
- What foods does your child like? dislike?
- Describe your child's sleeping and napping schedule.
- How do you put your child to sleep?
- Does your child share a bedroom? If so, with whom?
- Does your child sleep in the same bed as someone else? If so, with whom?
- How does your child relax or soothe herself?
- What are your child's favorite activities?
- How do you discipline your child?
- How do you handle the following situations?
    toilet training
    sharing
    messy play (paints, sand, water)
    sex roles
    racial concerns
- Who does your child play with at home?
- What are your child's responsibilities at home?
- What rules does your child follow at home?
- Is there anything else you would like to tell us about your child?

Family Culture

- What is your ethnic or cultural background?
- How do you identify yourself?
- What languages are spoken in your home? with your extended family?
- How comfortable are you speaking and reading English?
- What traditions, objects, or foods symbolize your family?
- Why are these things important? What values or history do they represent?
- What is your church affiliation or religious background?
- What values do you want us to teach to your children?
- How can we validate and support your family's lifestyle here at the center?
- What heroes, celebrations, songs, stories, and toys could we include that would represent and support your cultural heritage?
- Does your family celebrate birthdays? If so, how?
- Would you be willing to come and share your family's ways of celebrating holidays with your child's class?

(Adapted from University of Minnesota Child Care Center enrollment forms.)

Home Visits

Home visits help teachers get to know children and their families in more personal ways. They also offer chances to meet other family members and increase your understanding of how the family lives. Visits should be brief, lasting no more than 30 minutes, and should be arranged ahead of time with the child's parent(s). As a teacher, keep in mind that some families may view home visits with caution and concern, especially if they have experienced negative visits from social workers, child protection workers, and other human service workers.

Ongoing Communication

Once a parent-program relationship has been established, it is crucial that teachers maintain open communication with parents. Staff need to talk with parents as often as possible, not just when a child is sick or having a particularly difficult day. Realize that some parents may be shy, timid, or just not accustomed to asking questions. Teachers can develop a warm, friendly, outgoing manner that will help parents feel accepted, valued, and welcome.

Because of complex schedules and multiple responsibilities, it may be difficult for staff to talk with each parent on a daily basis. Centers can send information home to keep parents informed of program activities. Bulletin boards can be used to inform parents of multicultural events in the community. Newsletters can feature articles about different families at the center, children's developing awareness of culture, ideas for multicultural activities to do at home, and highlights from multicultural activities that have recently taken place at the center.

Curriculum and Classroom Events

Parent involvement enhances a center's efforts to provide multicultural education. Parents can have input in many ways. They can participate on a personnel committee to see that a racial mix of staff members is hired and that interviews include questions about experiences with other cultures or teaching multicultural education to young children. Parents also can form a holiday/celebration committee to decide which holidays will be celebrated at the center and how they will be celebrated. Parents may also enjoy planning and participating in celebrations, such as the observance of Martin Luther King, Jr.'s birthday, Cinco de Mayo, or the Hmong New Year. Parents could also volunteer in their child's classroom or be invited to share their cultural heritage with their child's class. A parent resource center could be established with multicultural books, records, and tapes for parents to borrow. Finally, programs could offer a parent support group to help parents explore their own heritage and attitudes toward ethnicity.

Conclusion

It is clear that culture influences families and their childrearing practices. As a result, culture influences what happens in your classroom. Apply the information in this chapter to your caregiving and teaching practices. Are all babies left alone to play on the floor? Are all babies held the same way? When children cry because they don't want to sleep alone on their own cot are they ignored? Are you sensitive to how difficult it is to get sand out of some children's hair? Do you pat children on the head or make them look you in the eye? Try to get to know each family individually. Expect that each family will be different based on their experience, values, lifestyle, and feelings about their cultural heritage.

Questions to Ponder

1. How did your ancestors come to America? Why did they come? What were their hopes and fears? Did they come alone or with other family members? Did they long to return to their homeland?
2. What role does culture and ethnicity play in your life?
3. What do you need to feel accepted and valued as an individual?
4. What changes can you make in your classroom (or entire program) to provide care and early education that is culturally responsive to the families you serve?

Resources and References

Crawley, Brenda. "Black Families in a Neo-Conservative Era." *Family Relations* 37 (1988): 415-19.

Fantini, Mario D. and Rene Cardenas, eds. *Parenting in a Multicultural Society*. New York: Longman,Inc., 1980.

Hamner, Tommie J., and Pauline H. Turner. *Parenting in Contemporary Society*. Englewood Cliffs, NJ: Prentice-Hall, 1985.

London, Harlan, and Wynetta Devore. "Layers of Understanding: Counseling Ethnic Minority Families." *Family Relations* 37 (1988): 310-14.

Martinez, Estella A. "Child Behavior in Mexican American/Chicano Families: Maternal Teaching and Childrearing Practices." *Family Relations* 37 (1988): 275-80.

McGoldrick, Monica, John Pearce, Joseph Giordano, eds. *Ethnicity and Family Therapy*. New York: Guilford Press, 1982.

Miller, Darla Ferris. *First Steps Toward Cultural Difference: Socialization in Infant/Toddler Day Care*. Washington DC: Child Welfare League of America, Inc., 1989.

Phillips, Carol Brunson. "Nurturing Diversity For Today's Children and Tomorrow's Leaders." *Young Children* (January 1988): 42-7.

———. "The Movement of Afro-American Children through Socio-Cultural Contexts: A Case of Conflict Resolution." *Anthology of Early Childhood Multicultural Education*. Edited by Clark Webb. Provo, UT: Brigham Young University Press, 1982.

Powell, Douglas R. *Families and Early Childhood Programs*. Washington, DC: National Association for the Education of Young Children, 1989.

Seifert, Kelvin L., and Robert J. Hoffnung. *Child and Adolescent Development*. Boston: Houghton Mifflin, 1987.

Staples, Robert. "The Emerging Majority: Resources for Nonwhite Families in the United States." *Family Relations* 37 (1988): 348-54.

CHAPTER 9

Talking to Children About Differences

The birth of language is one highlight of the years from two to seven. By the time children leave this period of development, they can carry on conversations, write words, and read simple books. It's language—learning to put words to one's thoughts and beliefs, saying those thoughts out loud for others to hear, expressing feelings with words rather than the body, and asking for wants and needs—that sets young children apart from infants. As a result, we talk to children and encourage children to talk to each other, and ask children to use words to name objects, request help, express feelings, relate life experiences, and organize their thinking. Since language is so critical to early childhood education, it is important to understand the power of words.

The Power of Words

> *"Sticks and stones may break my bones,*
> *but names can never hurt me."*
> *—Unknown*

Sociolinguistics is the study of how language is used in social situations. This field identifies the power of language in promoting and maintaining the social order.

As a system of naming and symbolizing, language may perpetuate social discrimination. Language, whether it is a name or a word, has the power to deny differences, to define, devalue, defame, and to make disappear. Phrases like "melting pot," "We are all the same," and "You are just like me" deny the differences between people. In addition, they very subtly use Euro-American values as the norm—the point of reference. Underneath these statements are such messages as: "You are just as good as a white person," and "Don't feel bad; you are just like us white people."

Slang expressions that describe and devalue minorities originate with the dominant culture. Names like *wop, pollack, jigaboo, highslant, spic, beaner, frog,* and *russkie* exemplify how words defame people. Often profanity is combined with these slang expressions to increase the negative impact.

Language also has the power to make someone disappear. Many immigrants to this country were afraid that their ethnic name would prevent them from opportunities and success in the United States. So they changed their name in order to fit in and be less conspicuous. People become culturally invisible when they exchange their ethnic surname for a more "American" one.

While words can defame and devalue people, they can also be used as tools for empowerment. People experience empowerment when they claim their own identity and name themselves. As individuals we empower ourselves when we express ourselves and our own uniqueness with words.

A Word About the Power of Silence

First they came for the Jews
and I did not speak out—
because I was not a Jew.
Then they came for the communists
and I did not speak out—
because I was not a communist.
Then they came for the trade
unionists and I did not speak out—
because I was not a trade unionist.
Then they came for me—
and there was no one left
to speak out for me.
        —Pastor Niemoeller (victim of the Nazis)

Silence has incredible power and is not always positive, as this quote from Pastor Niemoeller illustrates. Family members often use silence to hurt one another. A parent may use the "silent treatment" as an expression of anger and a form of punishment. The parent may not talk to the child for a day or two, leaving the child not knowing what she did wrong or knowing a way back to reconciliation.

Silence is also used when families have a "no-talk" rule about certain subjects. Maybe it's Uncle Harry's alcoholism, grandma's first marriage, or Auntie Sue's baby that died years ago. Sometimes the "no-talk" rule is applied to topics like sex, politics at the dinner table, or racism. Some family members know the truth about these situations. Perhaps everyone in the family knows what really happened, but these topics are never discussed at family gatherings or in public.

Even our country has "no-talk" rules. It's not acceptable to question and discuss whether or not Christopher Columbus discovered America, whether or not the Pilgrims and Indians really had a Thanksgiving feast, or whether the CIA and FBI were involved in the assassination of Dr. Martin Luther King, Jr.

Teachers and schools create "no-talk" rules for classrooms. Controversial situations occur, and questionable things are said or done. A Euro-American child calls a Native American child a "dumb Indian." Three boys in the block corner won't let a Laotian boy join them. They chant, "Go away, poopy boy. You talk funny." Everyone in the classroom hears it and sees it. Children may even look at each other as the situation occurs but nothing is said then or thereafter.

Many times, people feel paralyzed and make no response. Child care workers have told us that they fail to act because they are uncertain of the

right thing to say; or they fear making a mountain out of a molehill; or because they feel they should not be influencing children with their ideas (Ariel and others 1987, 24).

But the silence only serves to reinforce the hurt, pain, fear, hatred, and distorted thinking.

Agent for Change

Language is an integral part of social movements. Paulo Freire, who has written about the relationship between education and social liberation, believes that no group—whether it is an ethnic group, a social class, a generation, or a gender—can take up a struggle for liberation without having its own language (Freire 1985). For example, the ecology movement has brought words like *ecology, environment, pollution, toxic waste,* and *recycling* into everyday language. Each movement creates its own language that becomes part of the movement.

Early childhood programs and teachers show respect for minority groups' struggle for liberation and equality in this country when they identify them by the name their culture has chosen. Understand that frequently, names of cultural groups change with time and their movement toward identity, respect, and equality. For example, *Afro-American* was popular in the seventies whereas *Black American* or *African American* are currently used to define people of African descent. In addition, each individual may have a preferred way of being culturally defined. When in doubt, ask.

Empowering Children Through Language

Schools are places of empowerment when they allow and encourage children to speak words used in their home and daily life rather than the artificial, formal, "official" language at school. Traditionally, schools have forced children to use "correct English" when they speak and write. Few teachers have been willing to recognize or learn about ethnic language. In recent years, researchers have supported the belief that ethnic dialects like Black English or ebonics are legitimate and complete forms of English in their own right.

Using Words to Express Feelings

Helping others acquire words for self-expression is also an act of empowerment. A child gains power over fear when he has the words to describe the inner feeling and the object or situation that causes the fear. A sensitive adult can observe the child and follow up with responses such as

"I'm wondering if you are feeling scared?" or "What's scary for you today?" Sensitive listening and respectful responses empower children. Sensitive or reflective listening means listening to the child with full attention, looking for facial expressions, body language, and words that tell you how the child is feeling, and then acting like a mirror to accurately reflect back to the child their thoughts and feelings. Reflective listening empowers the child because it puts words to the child's experience. Respectful responses give children clear messages without verbally attacking or shaming them. Both respectful responses and reflective listening bring the unknown (and therefore uncontrollable) back down to life in a manageable and knowable form. Here are some examples of ways to respond to children that respect the child and encourage the child's self-expression:

Name feelings. "You look really sad, Juan. It hurt your feelings when Daniel called you 'brown skin'."

Express empathy. "Gee, Damani, I know just how you feel. It hurts when people call us names."

Voice your own feelings. "I'm uncomfortable with the way you are playing cowboys and Indians. I'm worried that you think Indians are bad guys that hurt people."

Respect the conflict and confusion. "It's hard to use your words when you are so upset."

Helping Children Expand Their Thinking

Just as sensitive listening and questioning demystify feelings, they can also be used to help children with their distorted thinking. Carolyn Pope Edwards, author of *Promoting Social and Moral Development in Young Children*, believes children need to dialogue with adults about their ideas in order to develop their social ideas and values. Dialogues are casual conversations between teachers and children. The word *dialogue* implies that the teacher and child are equals, sharing thoughts and ideas back and forth. They explore ideas together and learn from each other. Here are some of Edward's suggestions for expanding children's thinking:

1. Pay close attention to children while they are talking.
2. Set a calm, relaxed atmosphere so children have enough uninterrupted time in the conversation to form and express their ideas.
3. Affirm the thinking with comments like: "I believe you."
4. Clarify the thinking by repeating the idea back to the child using some of her key words and phrases.
5. Offer supportive, thought-provoking comments such as: "Gee, that's an interesting idea," "What makes you think that?" "Does anybody

else have an idea?" "Once somebody told me..." "What do you think of that idea?" "Maybe we could ask Carlos about this."

6. Avoid evaluating children's ideas by saying "good idea" or "good solution," because it gives children the impression that there is one right answer and that you are looking for the child to find the one right answer.

Responding to Children's Questions

Children become confused when things aren't talked about in the open. When differences between people are not acknowledged, they become mysterious, bigger than life, and even frightening. Young children are naturally curious and observant. These are the question-asking years. Young preschoolers constantly ask, "What's that?" Older preschoolers ask, "Why?" As adults we have four possible responses to children's questions about differences among people and lifestyles.

Put Downs. We can put children down for asking socially inappropriate questions. If we make them ashamed enough times, they will stop asking the questions and stop talking about the differences they notice. "Janice, that's not a nice thing to say." "Martin, don't you ever say that again." "Hilary, we don't talk about those things in public."

Ignore Them. We can ignore their questions by looking away and responding with silence, which results in treating children as though they don't exist.

Stereotype. We can answer their questions with myths, stereotypes, and lies: "Yes, Yolanda, that's a Black man and you'd better be careful because he might hurt you." "Stay away from Emilio; he comes from a poor, dirty family.

Accurate Information. We can answer their questions with simple, honest, accurate information: "Yes, Pham's skin is darker than yours and her eyes are shaped differently. She looks like her mom and dad, just like you look like your mom and dad."

Answering children's questions with accurate information is important because it shows approval of their questions, helps them feel acknowledged as a person, and helps them feel comfortable with differences. Children's questions also provide adults with a marvelous opportunity to ". . .affirm diversity and correct children's distorted, incorrect thinking due to stereotypes, myths, omission, distortion" (Morris 1987, 3).

General Guidelines. Children's questions often catch adults unaware. Redirect stereotypical negative thinking by giving accurate information and conveying an attitude of valuing differences.

Here are some guidelines for responding:
1. Always correct misinformation or incorrect assumptions.
2. Be sure you understand the question the child is asking.
3. Don't ignore children's fears—address them.
4. Don't delay in responding to a question, fear, or inaccurate information.
5. Examine your own behavior and language (Crary 1987, 18).

Responding to Discriminatory Behavior

If we are to create programs where every child and staff member is valued, we must learn to confront discriminatory behavior. This means immediately responding to children's discriminatory statements and behavior whether it is intentional or not.

Responding Actively

The following strategies for interrupting discriminatory behavior were compiled by Patricia DeRosa, MPCE Program Director, and are taken from *Cultural Links: A Multicultural Resource Guide.*
1. Don't ignore it. Do not let an incident pass without remark. To do so gives the message that you are in agreement with such behavior or attitudes. If the intervention would jeopardize the safety of the children, it should not take place at the exact time or place of the incident but it must be brought up as soon as appropriate.
2. Explain and engage when raising issues. Avoid preaching or being self-righteous.
3. Don't be afraid of possible tension or conflict. In certain situations, this may be unavoidable. These are sensitive and deep-seated issues that won't change without some struggle. Try to model for children that constructive conflict can be positive and resolved.
4. Be aware of your own attitudes, stereotypes, and expectations, and be open to discovering the limitations they place on your perspective. We are all victims of our misconceptions to some degree, and none of us remain untouched by the discriminatory images and behaviors we have been socialized to believe.
5. Project a feeling of understanding, love, and forgiveness when events occur. Don't guilt trip.
6. Recognize that you may become frustrated. Discriminatory behavior won't be eradicated in a day or from one "multicultural presentation." Sometimes things may seem to get worse before they get

better. Change or growth is a constant process, even in a supportive environment.

7. Be aware of your own hesitancies to intervene in these situations. Confront your own fears about interrupting discrimination; set your priorities and take action.

8. Be a role model. Always reflect and practice the positive values you are trying to teach. Don't compartmentalize your responses to "multicultural time."

9. Be nonjudgmental but know the bottom line. Issues of human dignity, equality, and safety are non-negotiable.

10. Distinguish between categorical thinking and stereotyping. For example, "redheads" is a category; but "redheads have fiery tempers" is a stereotype.

Reprinted with permission: *Cultural Links* is published and distributed by the Multicultural Project, Inc. Send prepaid orders ($12.50/ind. or $15/org.) to: MPI, 186 Lincoln Street, Boston, MA 02111.

In addition to the preceding guidelines, you may want to try some of these specific responses that have been adapted from a wonderful book on adult-child communication called *How to Talk So Kids Will Listen and Listen So Kids Will Talk* by Adele Faber and Elaine Mazlish:

1. Protest: "I don't like it when you call Marcus "Blackie." That's name-calling and it hurts his feelings."

2. Check thinking for accuracy: "People's skin comes in different colors."

3. Describe the behavior you want: "In our room we all play with one another. You may choose who to play with but you may not leave someone out of your play because of how they look or how they talk."

4. Help problem-solve and set limits: "Fabrizio wants to play with you again. If you two play together, what will you need to feel safe?"

5. Do something: "Mariah, I took the book you brought to school today off the book shelf because it has pictures of people that are untrue and unfair."

6. Encourage decision-making: "Chidi, you can either play with Kamii or you can tell her that you want to play with Sarah right now."

7. Encourage cooperation: "What's going on?" "Hmmm, how can we work this out so you are both happy?"

8. Tell children what you expect: "Circle time is a time for our whole class to be together. Everyone gets to be here in the circle."

9. Use visual displays: Draw or cut out a picture of children playing Indians. With a felt-tip marker, draw a large "X" through it. Draw or

cut out a picture of children playing together cooperatively. Put the two side-by-side for the children to see.

Taking Advantage of "Teachable Moments"

Opportunity to expand or clarify children's thinking, reinforce their positive behavior, and confront their discriminatory behavior happens at a moment's notice. Such is the case when a child arrives at school wearing a T-shirt with a stereotypical cartoon of a Native American, or when one child calls another derogatory names just as you are trying to get the class to finish cleaning up the room and come together for group time. These "teachable moments" are unplanned, spontaneous events. As a result, they can be very powerful teaching tools. They are life situations in which the child or children are the subjects of study. This is why these spontaneous interventions and conversations have so much potential for helping children redefine themselves and their place in the world.

Teacher Skills

In order to be successful, these spontaneous conversations require many things from teachers.

1. Teachers must be flexible and spontaneous, welcoming the questions and interruptions. An attitude of willingness to "go with the flow" means the adult will be ready to stop whatever she was doing in order to attend to a child or small group of children.

2. Teachers must be able to respond off the cuff to children's questions and discriminatory incidents in the classroom. A teacher can't carry around a script or rehearsed speech of what to say. At these moments we have to reach down inside of ourselves and speak from our innermost beliefs about what is right and true. When teachers speak from their life experience, they communicate strong feelings and conviction. There is power when the words convey the feelings that, "I care about this," "This is important to me," and "From my experience I know this to be true." *Roots & Wings* does not contain a script for every possible situation a teacher may encounter, because teachers need to find their own voices. They need to learn to phrase their explanations, requests, and praise in their own unique way.

3. Teachers must demonstrate the courage to confront children's biases and provide them with accurate information. This ability comes from having confronted one's own biases, misconceptions, and fears. Explore your own cultural roots. Examine your own fears, misconceptions, and stereotypes of people different from yourself. The

more aware you are of your own ethnic heritage and racism the more you will be able to teach and talk with children about people and culture. The two go hand-in-hand.

4. Teachers must examine and clean up their own language. What racial slurs taint your language? What racial jokes or stereotypes roll off your tongue? Be aware of all the subtle connotations with colors. The color white is used almost exclusively as a positive adjective while black is negative. For example: *white knight, white lie, white as snow; black sheep, black as night, black cat, or black as the ace of spades.* When we describe an issue in dualistic terms we say, "It's black or white," rather than "either or." Letty Cottin Pogrebin says, "If we leave language untouched, we won't ever really change anything. If however, we change the words we use, everything will change" (Pogrebin, 1980, 538).

One Day. . .
Youngsters will learn words they will not understand.
Children from India will ask:
What is hunger?
Children from Alabama will ask:
What is racial segregation?
Children from Hiroshima will ask:
What is the atomic bomb?
Children at school will ask:
What is war?
You will answer them.
You will tell them:
Those words are not used any more,
Like stagecoaches, galleys, or slavery—
Words no longer meaningful.
That is why they have been removed from dictionaries.
                              —*Martin Luther King, Jr.*

Questions to Ponder

1. When have people discriminated against or been judgmental toward you? How did you feel? How did you respond?
2. Can you think of a time when a child made a discriminatory remark? How did you respond? Would you respond differently if a similar incident happened today? If so, what would you say and do?

3. What are your questions or concerns regarding responding to children's discriminatory remarks and behavior?
4. Examine your language. What racial or ethnic slurs do you use?

Resources and References

Ariel, Marie Schacter, Val Hinderlie, Mary McCullough, Patricia Simmons, and Shelli Wortis. "Caring for Children in a Social Context: Eliminating Racism, Sexism and Other Patterns of Discrimination." *Cultural Links: A Multicultural Resource Guide.* Edited by Angela M. Giudice and Shelli Wortis. Boston: The Multicultural Project for Communication and Education, Inc., 1987.

Blood, Margaret A. "A Mission Possible." *Cultural Links: A Multicultural Resource Guide.* Edited by Angela M. Giudice and Shelli Wortis. Boston: The Multicultural Project for Communication and Education, Inc., 1987.

Crary, Elizabeth. "Talking About Differences Kids Notice." *Alike and Different: Exploring Our Humanity with Young Children,* Edited by Bonnie Neugebauer. Redmond, WA: Exchange Press, 1987.

Edwards, Carolyn Pope. *Promoting Social and Moral Development in Young Children: Creative Approaches for the Classroom.* New York: Teachers College Press, 1986.

Faber, Adele and Elaine Mazlish. *How to Talk So Kids Will Listen and Listen So Kids Will Talk.* New York: Avon Books, 1980.

Freire, Paulo. *The Politics of Education.* South Hadley: Bergin and Garvey, 1985.

Morris, Jeanne B. "Classroom Methods and Materials." *Understanding the Multicultural Experience in Early Childhood Education.* Edited by Olivia N. Saracho and Bernard Spodek. Washington DC: NAEYC, 1983.

Pogrebin, Letty Cottin. *Growing Up Free Raising Your Child in the 80's.* New York: Bantam Books, 1981.

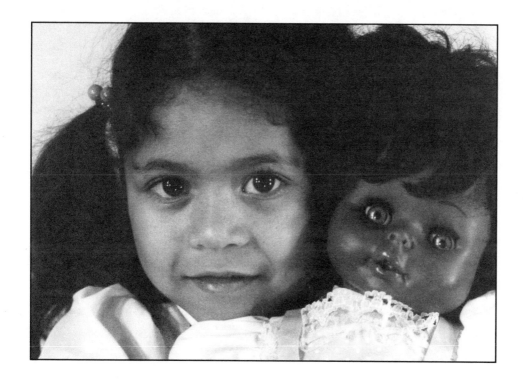

Other Toys 'n Things Press Publications

Basic Guide to Family Day Care Record Keeping — Clear instructions on keeping necessary family day care business records.

Calendar-Keeper — Activities, family day care record keeping, recipes and more. Updated annually. Most popular publication in the field.

Child Care Resource & Referral Counselors & Trainers Manual — Both a ready reference for the busy phone counselor and a training guide for resource and referral agencies.

The Dynamic Infant — Combines an overview of child development with innovative movement and sensory experiences for infants and toddlers.

Family Day Caring magazine — The best source of information on every aspect of home-based child care.

Family Day Care Tax Workbook — Updated every year, latest step-by-step information on forms, depreciation, etc.

Heart to Heart Caregiving: A Sourcebook of Family Day Care Activities, Projects and Practical Provider Support — Excellent ideas and guidance written by an experienced provider.

Kids Encyclopedia of Things to Make and Do — Nearly 2,000 art and craft projects for children aged 4-10.

Open the Door, Let's Explore — Full of fun, inexpensive neighborhood walks and field trips designed to help young children.

Parents of Young Children: A Parent Education Curriculum — A parent education curriculum; comprehensive 10-session class guide.

Practical Solutions to Practically Every Problem: The Early Childhood Teacher's Manual — Hundreds of proven and appropriate solutions for all your sticky problems.

S.O.S. Kit for Directors — Offers range of brainstormed solutions to everyday questions and problems.

Sharing in the Caring — Packet with provider/parent contracts, parent information and developmental guide.

Staff Orientation in Early Childhood Programs — Complete manual for orienting new staff on all program areas.

Survival Kit for Early Childhood Directors — Solutions, implementation steps and results to handling difficulties with children, staff, parents.

Teachables From Trashables — Step-by-step guide to making over 50 fun toys from recycled household junk.

Teachables II — Similar to *Teachables From Trashables;* with another 75-plus toys.

Those Mean Nasty Dirty Downright Disgusting but... Invisible Germs — A delightful story that reinforces for children the benefits of frequent hand washing.

Trusting Toddlers: Planning for One to Three Year Olds in Child Care Centers — Expert panel explains how to set up toddler program that really works.